SWEAT THE SMALL STUFF!

SWEAT THE SMALL STUFF!

RAM LOKAN

NEW DEGREE PRESS

SWEAT THE SMALL STUFF!

ISBN

978-1-63676-621-8 *Paperback*

978-1-63676-299-9 *Kindle Ebook*

978-1-63676-300-2 *Digital Ebook*

Papa, thank you for teaching me how to learn by doing.

Mama, thank you for teaching me how to learn with my heart.

CONTENTS

———

LIST OF CHARACTERS

Neha Wife
Nijhad Business Partner, Friend
Amir Former Owner

GREEN LEAF ORGANIZATIONAL CHART

Head Office

Balendra Finance & Accounts	**Kondo** Information Technology	**Samir** Warehouse	**Kabir** Procurement	**Sandra** Pricing

Store Management

Ali Peninsula	**Jeremy** Kimweri	**Mo** Bongoyo	**Godfrey** Arusha	**Marcus** Bakery	**Musa** Butchery

Neema Assistant Manager	**Amina** Receiving Manager

Sandeep Receiving Manager	**Rehema** Cashier

The stories in this book reflect my best recollection of events. Some names, locations, and identifying characteristics have been changed to protect the privacy of those depicted. Dialogue has been re-created from memory.

INTRODUCTION

———

Have you ever had one of those moments where you look around and wonder, "What am I doing with my life?"

For me, that moment came in March 2016. I was bagging groceries in a supermarket chain I had just purchased in Dar es Salaam, Tanzania when a customer yelled at me for crushing her lettuce by putting it at the bottom of her shopping bag.

Now I knew I had a lot to learn about the business, but bagging groceries? I couldn't even do *THAT* correctly? Needless to say, the life of a grocery store titan was not starting off as well as I thought it would.

After three apologies and the embarrassing involvement of the cashier and store manager, this regular customer left, but not before clearly expressing doubts about my future in the supermarket industry. Little did she know that at that exact moment, I was having those same doubts myself.

There I was, having graduated top of my high school, graduated with honors from McGill University in Canada, graduated again with honors from Harvard Business School just five years prior, having worked at some of the largest banks and financial institutions in the United States and

India... failing at bagging lettuce in a grocery store. How did my life get so far off track?

Well, believe it or not, it was all part of the plan.

* * *

Of my graduating class at Harvard Business School, more than 75 percent went into either financial services, consulting, or technology, earning six-figure salaries. By that time, some were even earning in the seven-figure range. They were negotiating multi-billion-dollar deals at Blackstone, strategizing about the future of e-commerce at McKinsey, or building Airbnb in Asia. That is the expected path to pursue when you graduate from a top business school: big deals in big places.

And that's what I did too... at first. Right after school, I moved to India in 2011 and joined a real estate private equity fund. I thought that was the place to learn and immerse myself in business. It was, to an extent, but my most important lesson came not from negotiating a deal with a difficult counterparty or meeting with investors and describing the deep analysis we had done on our latest investment. No, the most invaluable guidance I ever got was at dinner in India on a cold January night.

As I did multiple times a year, I took our investors and advisors on a tour of the various properties the fund owned across the country. In Udaipur, we spent the day touring hotels and the evening debriefing over a meal. During this dinner, I happened to sit next to Professor Segel, my Harvard real estate professor and an advisor to the fund. He was describing where he was in his career at my age, right after the big Savings & Loan crisis that left bankrupt a myriad of commercial properties across the United States.

Convincing a few investors to put down startup capital, he went around the country purchasing small, run-down properties for pennies on the dollar on the hunch that if he spent time, money, and effort renovating them, they would be worth more than he'd paid. He was right about the profits, but boy did he put in the effort. He was traveling most of the time and working relentlessly.

"Did you enjoy yourself?" I asked.

"I loved every minute of it! Those were the best times of my life, and I probably learned more in those few years than anything I ever learned at school."

He told me about how he bought the wrong properties in the wrong parts of town after being oversold their value by very convincing brokers and how he tried to turn them around. He was losing cash on one of his properties, but because he was honest and transparent with his banker, they gave him time to work it out. And he told me how many times he got rejected by potential investors, tenants, and brokers and how he learned to identify the real risks of each deal.

I was fascinated by his stories, and if I'm honest, a little jealous. I remember thinking just before dinner that I was on a clear path to learning business. Now I was being inspired to rethink that assessment. Professor Segel did all those things when he was around my age, during the early days of his career, and he had to do everything himself—find deals, negotiate them, arrange financing, manage properties, deal with tenants, etc. That's when he worked the hardest, toiling every day to make sure his properties would return a profit to his investors, but that's also when he enjoyed himself the most. He learned the business, and he gleaned life-long lessons that he still shares to this day.

So I started asking myself some tough questions: Should I be doing what I'm doing now? Am I doing the right things to further my learning? What else could I be doing now to become an effective business leader?

Out of all the stories he shared that night, two lessons stood out:

1. Work at a small, growing company; you get to do things and have responsibilities you "don't deserve."

2. Typical MBA graduates don't get their hands dirty. If you are committed to learning, go into leasing or property management, where you have to do and learn everything yourself.

Those lessons taught him a sense of responsibility and ownership, and how different departments in a company interact with one another to create value and grow.

"Do something small." Now, that's not the typical advice you hear as a graduate from one of the most prestigious schools in the world.

How are we supposed to do something small when the signing bonus from the big firms that hire you right out of school is enough to buy a car or put a deposit on a house? People do not pay you car-money in signing bonuses expecting you to come in and "do something small." No, they expect earth-shattering advice and analyses gleaned from your years of experience and exposure to some of the brightest business minds you could ever meet, such as the late Harvard Business School professor Clayton Christensen.

His Innovator's Dilemma theory—that big successful companies neglect potential customers at the lower end of their market and are, thus, ripe for disruption from smaller, nimbler competitors—shaped the strategies of late Apple CEO Steve Jobs and was responsible for turning around Intel.[1] There's nothing small about such an idea. Doing something small after studying at a place so big would be anathema to everything it stands for.

After hearing my former professor talk about his early experiences, I had an intuition of what I needed to do. I had to get my hands dirty and sweat what would look to others like small stuff. I needed to learn business by struggling with its nuts and bolts and learning from the people involved at every level.

Marked by the words I heard that night, I knew I needed to take a detour from the common post-MBA path I was following.

So when an opportunity came, I bought a supermarket chain in Dar es Salaam and moved from New York to run it. I did all the seemingly small things alongside the team to understand how the business ran and put into practice all those courses we were taught in business school. I saw what the real life of a business owner was all about from the ground up.

Was it worth leaving a city I loved for the complete unknown? A country I had never been to, a continent I barely understood, and an industry I wasn't familiar with?

Yes, a million times yes. It was the best thing I ever did. I learned to love business not for its big moments but for all its spirit and the people in it. And today, it has made me a better businessperson, manager, and investor. I get to put into practice daily what I learned during those years running a supermarket chain in East Africa.

---

1   Clayton M. Christensen, *The Innovator's Dilemma: When New Technologies Cause Great Firms to Fail* (Boston: Harvard Business Publishing, 1997).

This is a story about what a customer complaint on the price of corn flakes teaches you about the logistics of a supply chain spanning nine countries; how promoting a cashier earns the trust of all the employees; why designing uniforms and wearing a name tag helps everyone feel like you're part of the same company; and why showing up at the bakery at 4:00 a.m. makes you a better leader.

In the life of any business, there are three phases: learn, manage and grow, and sell.

Through my experience, we will explore those three phases. I will share stories that shaped my journey in each of those key moments and give you tips on what I learned along the way.

I will also share thoughts on my journey as an entrepreneur, what I learned from it, and how it has helped me grow.

Ultimately, I want to show you how sweating the small stuff made me look at business in a new light and led to the company's success and my personal growth.

Whether you are an ambitious college graduate thinking about your first job or an experienced professional wondering about your next move, I hope this book will give you a different perspective on what it takes to be successful in business.

Hint: You don't need to move to Africa and run a grocery store.

But you do need to listen to everyone in and around your business. From the truck drivers to the accountants, the customers to your suppliers, they all add critical viewpoints to your business, and you need to learn and process that information. And yes, you even need to learn that lettuce, like eggs, should be packed at the top of the grocery bag. Focusing on the small things ultimately teaches you the most, and that will make you a better businessperson in the long run.

PART 1

LEARN

"You need to sweat a little to learn a lot."

CHAPTER 1

MY FIRST ATTEMPT

———

After hearing Professor Segel, I started reviewing where my career was going and thought I needed to make some changes. It took me some time to figure out exactly what, but like Siddhartha Gautama's teachings, his words kept resonating and lighting the path ahead.

While attending a wedding a few months later, I met a friend of a friend I hadn't seen in a long time. He was working for a small real estate family office in the United States and I started peppering him with questions.

"What sectors are attractive right now?"

"Well, at the moment, with interest rates being so low, all sectors are attractive, but we like to buy run-down properties that need to be fixed up and sold later at a profit."

"Do you think residential or commercial properties are most lucrative?"

"It really depends on which market you are in. In some cities, residential is on fire; in others, you have a clear lack of offices; and in others still, retail centers are booming."

"Which cities do you think are the most lucrative nowadays?"

"Honestly, anything that's not New York or San Francisco. Those two markets are too pricey, but you see growth almost everywhere else. Why, what are you getting at?"

"I'm thinking of going into investing and managing real estate on my own. This is really helping me get a lay of the land."

Our conversation triggered his thinking hat. In between wedding toasts and dinner courses, we spent a few hours discussing and narrowing down opportunities in the United States for an investor like me. More than anything, this conversation convinced me that I should go out there and do my own investments.

* * *

In the spring of 2014, I left my job investing in real estate in India and moved to Houston, Texas, where I was ready to invest in residential and retail properties. Armed with a few contacts from my friend, my Harvard network, and a lot of zeal to succeed, I was ready to use this city as a launching pad!

* * *

Three out of four venture-backed startups fail, according to research by Shikhar Ghosh, a Harvard Business School lecturer. Ghosh also found that more than 95 percent of startups fall short of their initial projections.[2] I knew the stats but told myself I would do better.

---

2 Carmen Nobel, "Why Companies Fail—and How Their Founders Can Bounce Back," *Harvard Business School Working Knowledge,* March 7, 2011.

I was used to speaking with institutional investors with billions of dollars to deploy around the globe and doing deal sizes of $50m+. I figured that starting a bit smaller should make things easier. Little did I know how wrong I was! With help from my network, I started understanding the city and what drove its growth. Eventually, I was put in touch with a residential real estate broker, Jerry, who soon became my new best friend.

Jerry and I met four days a week always at 9:00 a.m. at the same coffee shop near the intersection of the Grand Parkway and Highway 290. We established a clear routine for the days we met. The afternoon prior, he sent me a list of thirty or so properties for sale with all its details and photos. I had to sift through them and identify ten to fifteen houses we could visit. These were always in different neighborhoods so we'd get a feel for different parts of the city. This also helped with identifying promising commercial opportunities.

* * *

Jerry had been a residential broker in Houston for over twenty years. He was tall with short black hair and a well-groomed mustache. He met his wife in high school and immediately knew he would marry her. Having no money, he joined the military and spent a few years away before returning to Houston and fulfilling his promise to her with his savings. At the time, they moved just a few houses down from where he grew up. He fell into the brokerage business completely by accident.

One night, a friend convinced him to go to a seminar on flipping properties. The speaker had attracted a big crowd and showed off how he built his wealth by buying and flipping houses. And for a low price, this speaker was willing to divulge all his secrets so those in attendance could one day drive a Mercedes like his.

Jerry was skeptical about how one could get rich this way. Besides, he didn't have the capital to put up as equity to buy a house himself, but the size of the crowd that evening gave him an idea. What is the common link when buying and selling properties? Well, all the folks in the room would need a broker to help them get on with their business!

He spent his days driving around neighborhoods looking for properties for sale and his evenings going to seminars on house flipping, selling his services identifying good investment opportunities for the crowd. His first sale was a disaster. He didn't realize that being a broker is a regulated profession in the state of Texas and you need a license to practice and earn a commission. He did all the hard work, but another broker earned his fees.

Instead of putting him off, this experience convinced him even more that he needed to become a broker. After all, here he was doing all the work and someone else who did nothing besides sign a few papers earned a big commission.

He's learned a lot since but what made Jerry a good ally was that he also started flipping houses, so he knew to look at the investment value of a property. And he was intrigued about the commercial property game. We learned from each other. He explained how Houston had developed over the years and what made a "good" investment neighborhood vs. a "not-so-good" one.

Hint: look at the lawn, it must be just right. If it's completely untidy, it often means the neighborhood is full of families who work too hard to have time to take care of the lawn; they might struggle to pay rent on time. If the lawn is very tidy, it probably means the neighborhood families have gardeners to take care of their property and values will be expensive. The lawn must be just right.

In exchange, I walked him through the economics of owning a shopping center: how to evaluate it, how to manage tenants, etc. Of course, all those things I had learned from my desk evaluating investments for the fund where I worked, but still, the theoretical knowledge was there, and it was time to put it into practice.

I knew buying a grocery-anchored center was out of my price range. Those are your typical neighborhood malls with a Kroger, Target, or Walmart hypermarket as the anchor tenant, and in a straight line on both sides, you find a cellular service provider, fast food chains, banks, etc. Because of the size and the safe nature of the grocer, the properties would fetch a high price, above ten million dollars, with little room to improve and make profits in the short term.

Instead of those large centers, I looked at smaller properties. You often find strip centers adjacent to those big ones with little restaurants, laundry services, and other mom-and-pop shops. Nothing fancy, but that's why I targeted them. These properties benefit from being close to the big grocer, generally still at a strategic intersection, while being sold at a more affordable price. I wanted to buy properties under five million dollars, spend a little on maintenance to fix them up, raise the rent, and eventually generate a return on my investment of over 20 percent. Thus, my first investment criteria was born: well-located properties with mom-and-pop tenants that needed some Tender Loving Care.

Lesson #1: Be clear about your investment criteria.

I targeted all intersections in the neighborhoods I deemed attractive and, with a little more perseverance and luck, as Jerry and I were driving down Route 6 one day, I finally found a small strip center for sale in Sugar Land, Texas called

Kingdom Plaza. I hoped this would be my ticket to the fast-paced world of real estate investing.

Before leaving my previous professional life, my final deal was an investment in a luxury residential property worth more than $150 million. This strip center was listed for $3 million, so I thought, *This will be a piece of cake.* Hubris got the better of me.

* * *

The seller was a doctor in his sixties who used his savings to build the center ten years ago. During that time, he managed the tenants and property himself and now wanted to pay back his loan and retire. This now became my second investment criteria: find properties owned and managed by individual sellers. By doing everything themselves and with a day job, they often can't optimize the center as it should be.

Online, it looked like the property had been on sale for quite some time now, so I believed I had some leverage in negotiating. I met the doctor at the property, and he showed me around as we both sweated profusely on a hot, sunny Texas afternoon.

"Here you can see the paving is brand new. We just redid this last year and even put in a slope so the water flows away from the building when it rains."

"Makes sense," I said confidently, pretending I could identify one-year-old vs. ten-year-old pavement.

"You can see we repainted the entire building a few months ago. There are a few black spots on the side walls, but that's because of the grease from the restaurants. You can get them to fix that once you own the place."

"Yes, of course."

"This space here is empty. The previous tenant was late on rent, and I told him to leave. Plenty of people are looking to lease space, and I didn't want to have to deal with late payers. Better lease it to someone else. This will be great and easy for you to manage."

"Awesome!"

I clearly had no idea what I was doing and let myself be led around the center. I learned the hard way that even though the paving was recent, it was not high quality, no tenant ever pays to fix something outside their four walls, and finding good tenants who pay on time is extremely hard.

We quickly went on to negotiate the price.

The center was 55 percent leased, which meant three empty units that needed tenants. If I could find three tenants, just three, I could almost double the cash flow and, thus, the value of the property. The question was how much of that value I should pay upfront.

I had settled on paying $2.5 million, but the seller had in mind a sale price of $2.7 million to pay off his loan and retire; he wouldn't budge below that. This required paying more than I thought was fair and, frankly, I should have walked away at that point. I didn't.

I had moved to Houston almost five months ago and looked at hundreds of houses and dozens of such retail centers. It had been good learning, but tiring. More importantly, I wouldn't make money on learning, but on actually owning a property and fixing it.

I had come close before to acquiring another center, but I was too late. Someone else had already toured it, and before I could make up my mind, they bought it. It was emotionally draining to go through the excitement of almost owning a property that fits your criteria only to lose it at the last minute.

So when I finally had something that looked reasonably viable, I overestimated my skills, let my emotions get the better of me, and gave in to his price.

Mistake #1: Don't let emotions dictate the price.

I needed $2.7 million to buy the property and another $200,000 for fixing it. I planned to finance the transaction with a bank loan of $1.8 million, invest $100,000 of my savings, and tap into my network of family and friends to raise the remaining $1 million I needed to fund the purchase. Since everyone I knew was a) in finance, b) had substantial savings, and c) had an appetite to invest, I thought it would be easy to raise the funds.

I put together an investment memorandum and sent it to over thirty people. The analysis was good and the document well put together, thanks to my years of experience in the industry. And, indeed, I got quite a few people interested, just not enough to fund the entire equity.

I managed to only raise $900,000, short of what I needed, but because I was in a rush to close the deal, I thought, *No problem, this will be enough.* The extra funds were there as a buffer to cover expenses while I looked for three tenants. To remove that shortfall, I only had to convince myself it would take me much less time to find those tenants.

Mistake #2: Always raise more money than you think you need. And whatever you do, don't raise less.

Next up, I had to get a loan.

I first went to the banks I used personally, Citibank and JPMorgan. I was confident that years of having an account with both, never a late payment on my credit card, and what I thought was generally an unblemished track record of deposits and investments would lend me enough credence to secure a loan.

After hustling for weeks to meet the business account managers, I was squarely rejected. It turns out having a personal bank account meant nothing. For them, you are starting fresh on the business side—no track record, no business history, no loans. I was bummed.

When I moved to Houston, I started going to events for young real estate professionals. These were often meetings over drinks or planned happy hour events at a local restaurant. They were good occasions to meet other people in the industry and get to know the landscape. Early on, I met a loan officer from a local bank. When I shared my plan for acquiring commercial properties, he was keen on helping me finance them. That meeting had happened almost five months ago and I doubted he would remember me, but I was desperate.

I found his business card and called RJ from Houston Unity Bank (HUB). HUB is a local community bank, and despite being known for a conservative lending strategy, RJ's role was specifically to identify new clients to finance.

To my surprise, he remembered me. I told him about the deal I had on the table, and he was immediately interested. We agreed to meet the following day at the property and discuss it further.

The next morning, we met at the center and started the visit. Since the property was only about one thousand square meters, the tour lasted about fifteen minutes, after which we sat down and had coffee in the donut shop anchoring the property. I laid out my case for the acquisition, how I thought about the valuation, the types of tenants there currently, and who I thought we could get for the vacant spaces.

"We already have restaurants for dinner and a donut shop for breakfast. I think a sandwich and salad place would make sense so people can grab lunch here," I started.

"Ok, but there are already sandwich places in the center a few miles north and south of you. What makes you think this location would work better?" asked RJ.

"Well, I agree there is one south of here, but it's past the intersection, so they're missing out on that shop. And the one north of here is on the wrong side of the road when you consider where the offices are and which way commuters are traveling."

"Ok, and what about the corner space? That's a massive one, what's your plan?"

"For that one, I was thinking of a banqueting venue. There's nothing like that in the area and there is a big Indian community nearby. This would work well to host weddings and large functions."

"Such a venue will be expensive to fit out. Is that included in your business plan?"

I showed him my figures. He looked thoughtfully at my spreadsheet and continued asking questions.

"What rental have you assumed for the empty units?"

"Since they're less visible from the road, I took a 20 percent discount to the rental on the prime spaces."

"How long do you think it will take to lease out?"

"I assumed three months for the smaller ones, and between six and nine months for the banqueting area."

Finally, he looked up from my document.

"I think this is workable and the numbers make sense. I will write up your proposal and present it to our credit committee. Let's see what they say."

I couldn't believe it. I had gotten external validation on my work from someone I hardly knew, and whose job it was to look at such proposals and say *no* more often than not! However, my initial excitement quickly faded when RJ called me a week later with an update.

In previous transactions I was involved, once you put together a loan package, the credit committee process was done in a black box, somewhere on the high floor of a giant tower of a global bank. The loan officer or your relationship banker would then call you with the good news. It was not the same process at HUB.

"Ram, the committee looked at your proposal and they had a few questions. And since you're a new client of the bank, they also would like to meet you in person."

In person? That sounds scary.

"Oh, ok, sure. What kind of questions?" I replied.

"I'm not sure, but don't worry. These guys have fifty years of Houston experience combined, so whatever they ask will only be to the benefit of the project."

Urgh, that's the end of this process...

I was done and would be exposed as a fraud. Their fifty years of Houston experience would overwhelm my five months. I told myself it was a good run, but for the sake of respecting RJ who had pushed my deal so hard, I had to go in front of the committee.

> **Lesson #2: Don't underestimate the importance of building relationships when starting a new business. Even a random connection can help, but it's still worth nothing if you don't put in the hard work and effort.**

* * *

My appointment was for a Wednesday morning at 10:30 a.m. I still remember the drive and how sweaty my hands were when I pulled up to HUB's headquarters. It was hot, but that was not why I was sweating. I was nervous as hell! My initial feelings of giving up gave way to some hope. That hope built into the nervousness I was experiencing. After all, if I thought I had no chance of getting a loan, I'd have no reason to be nervous, but perhaps somewhere deep inside, I knew I had a shot. My only shot. And I had to do my best; otherwise, I would regret it forever.

I arrived fifteen minutes early and sat in the parking lot for eight minutes so I wouldn't appear too eager. It gave me another chance to look through my business plan, run the figures in my head, and check that I had all the requisite documents along with my trusty calculator in case I was asked to adjust my projections and make new calculations on the spot.

I had memorized the area of the building, the area of the land, the names and lease terms of all the current tenants, the monthly expenses, the cash flows today, and my expectations once the empty spaces were taken up. I felt slightly better.

The boardroom where our meeting took place was located on the top floor. The building itself was not particularly high, being in the suburbs of Houston, but it was impressive nonetheless. You always feel an extra tinge of awkwardness mixed with pride when you are invited to the top floor of any building.

The elevator doors opened on a corridor filled with mahogany wood and emerald-colored carpeting. I felt awe-struck being there.

I walked into the boardroom and never before have I felt so important, humbled, and intimidated at the same time. Ten white-haired men, all dressed in grey or black suits with white shirts and ties, looked at me sternly. I was asked to sit at one end of the massive table while they all introduced themselves. RJ was sitting on the other end.

Once the introductions were done, the bank's CEO asked me to introduce myself and the opportunity. I did as asked, and over the next ten or so minutes, went into my planned acquisition of Kingdom Plaza. It felt very mechanical and rehearsed—because it was. I wrapped up that brief and asked if there were any questions. I couldn't read the room and didn't know if I had gotten people excited, scared, or confused.

Then one person asked more about my background. He wanted to know where I was brought up and what got me into Houston real estate. I hadn't rehearsed that, but I told them about my career so far and recounted how I met this professor who triggered my interest in entrepreneurship and real estate. They loved hearing it and kept asking more follow-up questions.

Next, they focused on how much of my net worth I was investing in this endeavor—over 50 percent of it, which turned out to be the right answer.

In the end, they were not so much worried about the plan itself. It was thoughtful and well put together. They wanted to see that I was fully committed, that I had "pain money" at stake. This meant that if the investment went sour, I would lose a substantial portion of my wealth. If I lost my family and friends' investment, it would hurt my relationships and reputation. In other words, they wanted to see if I was all in, understand my motivations, and whether I would push through when the going was tough. I was and it showed; my passion for this business made up for my lack of years and experience. That's what convinced the credit committee.

In a forty-five-minute meeting, I got a $1.8 million loan and could now close on Kingdom Plaza.

> **Lesson #3: People judge a book by more than its cover. Talk not only about your plan but also about yourself, what moves you, and why you are doing what you are doing.**

* * *

The day we closed the deal and I got the keys to the property, I was ecstatic. I went around to each tenant, introduced myself, gave them my freshly minted business card, and said, "Please call me anytime you need anything." I was earnest, but I never could have predicted I would have to manage my first crisis just hours later.

Turns out, I forgot to plan for a proper handover, and the previous owner switched off the electricity and water to the entire center the day we closed on the deal. I had to scramble and rush through an application to the local utilities to get power and water. It took a little over a day, but we got it done, and the tenants forgave my lack of planning after I again went around to everyone in earnest and explained what happened.

I hired a large professional leasing company with whom I had built a relationship during the previous months. They managed some of the biggest malls in the suburbs and were keen to participate in my growth story. It involved, however, managing more than one small strip center. They started off well and drew some interest for the empty spaces, but after a few weeks of marketing the property, and not seeing any traction on my end for more properties to manage, they reduced their efforts.

This was a big blow, but had I known better, it made sense. Why would they spend all their resources and efforts on this small property when they're dealing with national tenants who want to take multiple spaces in the best locations around town?

I didn't know what to do. On the one hand, I thought these guys should know best, and if they weren't getting anywhere, then perhaps I had made a mistake and this center was doomed to failure.

On the other hand, I couldn't believe that no one, absolutely no one, had come to visit the space even once to see if it was worth opening shop here. It didn't make sense.

I was losing sleep and getting anxious. What could I do next? Right after New Year's, I had to give an update to my investors. I was supposed to be well-advanced on my leasing plans. In theory, I should have even secured one of the three tenants by now. Instead, I had no tenants and no leads. It was an awful situation.

I resigned myself to the only option left: take over the leasing myself. After all, I planned to sweat the small stuff, so how could I let anyone else do this? Leasing is the core of property management, and who better than the owner to tout the virtues of the center than yours truly!

I needed a strategy once again. I targeted similar centers in adjacent neighborhoods with complementary tenants: medical offices, laundromats, clothing retailers, etc.

And in my update to investors, I was honest about what happened. I trusted a large firm to do the work and they let me down. I should have known better because this was too small to pique their interest, but all was not lost because I would do everything in my power to make this work.

> **Mistake #3: If you want something done and it's critical to your business, don't outsource it. Do it yourself!**

I spent days after days, weeks after weeks touring other centers, dropping my business card and center map to potential tenants, but came up short. There was some interest here and there, but no one seemed to be interested in expanding at the rentals I thought were fair. I overestimated mom-and-pop shops greatly. They preferred to run a single operation they could manage themselves and could not handle the logistics and money to open a second location.

Moreover, an oil crisis was brewing and Houston was beginning to feel the brunt of it.

Salvation came from the most unexpected (for me!) of places—my current tenants. I received a call from an unknown number one day. Before owning Kingdom Plaza, I would never answer those, but I had given my business cards to so many people that now I had to answer my phone at all times, hoping a tenant would come through.

This was indeed a lead. A couple who had another successful business wanted to open a small sandwich shop in the center.

Bingo!

This was exactly what I needed, and I loved their concept. When I met them, I asked my most pressing question.

"How did you hear about this property?"

"We know Rashida, the owner of the hair salon in the plaza. She's a good friend of ours. When we said we were looking to open a new business, she immediately recommended we call you."

This was music to my ears. I had taken such good care of the property in the last six months, been attentive to all the problems faced by the tenants, and reacted quickly to any issues arising; therefore, my tenants themselves were pushing for the center to be successful. I didn't even think about it, but they were as vested in Kingdom Plaza's success as I was!

Unbeknownst to me, they started spreading the word in their network that the new owner of the center took care of the property and was doing all the right things to promote it. Apparently, taking care of tenants was not so common in the property world.

That's how I met this couple and the other two tenants I needed to fill up the empty spaces, including a banquet hall. After a year of ups and downs, doing things I never thought I would do or was capable of handling, the center was full.

> **Lesson #4: Treat all your stakeholders with respect and they will take care of you.**

With the center full, I was now ready to start the last phase of my strategy: sell. I worked with a broker to advertise the center at a price I thought was fair given the new cash flow profile. It took a few months and some price reductions below my expectations, but we got someone to bite.

After three years of ownership, I made a small gain upon selling the center. Revamping the empty spaces ate significantly into my profit, but nevertheless, I had completed an important part of my investment journey. I made mistakes along the way but learned important, critical lessons for the adventure I was about to embark on.

> **Lesson #5: Make sure to write down all the mistakes you made along the way. That way you can avoid repeating them later!**

RAM'S TIPS:

- Be clear about your investment criteria. Take your time to do the research and figure out your competitive advantage.

- Don't let your emotions dictate the price.

- Always raise more money than you think you need. And whatever you do, don't raise less.

- Don't underestimate the importance of building relationships when starting a new business. Even a random connection can help, but it's nothing if you don't put in the hard work and effort.

- People judge a book by more than its cover. Talk not only about your plan but also about yourself, what moves you, and why you are doing what you are doing.

- If you want something done and it's critical to your business, don't outsource it. Do it yourself.

- Treat all your stakeholders with respect and they will take care of you.

- Make sure to write down all the mistakes you made along the way. That way you can avoid repeating them later!

CHAPTER 2

THE FIVE-YEAR REUNION

June 2016 was my five-year reunion with Harvard Business School. It also happened to be four months after I acquired Green Leaf Supermarket and moved to Dar es Salaam, Tanzania. How did I make that decision? I'll get to that...

Meanwhile in Boston, the excitement in the air was palpable not only because of my reunion but because throughout Boston, five-, ten-, twenty-, thirty-, and even seventy-year reunions were going on at the same time. The entire city was filled with the anticipation of reuniting with old friends and reminiscing about all the good times that had been shared.

Although everyone I knew was looking forward to this reunion, I dreaded it. I almost canceled going because I feared the judgment of my former classmates.

This was the first time I would expose the "Plan" on such a big scale, and I feared being mocked for it. Everyone always worries about going back to these reunions and feeling judged, but I thought my story was just a bit more out there. Of course, I had already shared the Plan with my close friends, who all supported it, but this was a different, much larger, and less personal crowd.

I kept picturing in my head how people would talk about me:

"Did you hear Ram moved to Tanzania?"

"TAN-zania? What is that? The Uber of tanning salons?"

"No, it's a country in Africa! I mean, why would he do that?"

I was *SO* nervous about explaining my new career choice. I was following a path, yes, but it looked very different from the traditional paths followed by my classmates. Explaining the route I was taking required more... explanation since I did not fit into any simple bucket. And it's not like you have time at these reunions to go through the details of your three-point plan and demonstrate how it fits into your long-term career.

It didn't help that around the time of the reunion, I started seeing my classmates mentioned in business magazines or even headlining news articles. "So-and-so is a Top 40 Under 40 Marketer." "You Wish You Sold Your Company at the Price She Did!" I even found one of my classmates in a home design magazine! "How to Have It All: Top Consultant Shows Us How to Design a Mid-Century Modern Home." Everyone was everywhere doing something cool, and I didn't think I would make the cut.

I kept imagining the awkwardness and silences that would accompany my upcoming conversations, so I rehearsed what I would say repeatedly. It went something like this:

"Hey, Ram! Long time no see. How are you?"

"Good, good. You? How are things?"

"Going well! Doing the same old since school. What are you up to these days? Last I heard, you were working at an investment fund in India."

"Well, yes, that was a while ago. I actually quit my job."

"Oh, really? And what are you doing now?"

"I know it sounds crazy, but... I bought a chain of supermarkets in Dar es Salaam and moved there a few months ago."

Then, still in my hypothetical conversation, I faced incredulous looks all around, along with complete silence and bewilderment. I would add a rushed explanation: "I want to become an expert investor in emerging markets, and to do so, I need to build the necessary skills. I have to do the small things, work hard at all jobs in a company, really sweat it out until I gain an intuition for business. So when this opportunity came up, I took the chance. I believe this will be the key to developing my investing skill set."

Once my short speech was done, I planned to quickly retreat to the bar or maybe even just head directly back to my hotel room to avoid any further embarrassment. At reunions, you typically categorize people into certain molds: successful, on the way to success, unsuccessful. Guess which bucket I would be thrown into?

For the classmates along my escape route who somehow wanted to know why exactly this was the right opportunity, I even prepared an elevator-pitch version of my plan describing its facets in more detail.

First, Green Leaf was an established business. It had been around for over twelve years, and I could learn all the tricks of the trade from the team. We had a Head of Finance & Accounts, a Procurement Manager, a Warehouse Manager— all people who had been with the business for years and had tons of experience for me to learn from.

Two, it was an old-school business—a brick-and-mortar store that generates positive cash flow. I could apply all the lessons learned in school about marketing, operations, finance, etc. and it would be directly relevant to the business. I would combine my education and past experience with the practical knowledge of the team to see how we could enhance customer satisfaction and profitability.

Three, it had potential. The country was growing, the region was growing, and the supermarket chain had a great reputation in the country. If I could figure out how to leverage that experience and expand the chain, we could do well. We would begin by improving the current operations, and then we could grow it throughout the region. Eventually, the Plan involved opening stores in other large cities in the country, and maybe even Nairobi or Kampala, the other capital cities of East Africa.

What I was doing would enable me to rapidly improve my business skills, turbocharge my learning, and, ultimately, lead me to become a better investor. It looked like a detour but was actually more of a shortcut.

Easy peasy!

> **Lesson #1: Don't be afraid to rehearse your plan and poke holes in them. It can help you fight that knot in your stomach.**

* * *

When I walked into the classroom, with a knot in my stomach and feeling hot and sweaty despite the cold air blowing, I bumped into probably the worst person I could going into this reunion: Gordon.

Gordon was a classic product of business school—tall, athletic, ultra-smart, and now working at a top private equity firm in New York. He was the archetype of who I thought would judge me for what I was doing and exactly the person I wanted to avoid at all costs as I was practicing my little update speech. I pictured him hearing the Plan and laughing out loud. Then he'd call others over to hear my story so they could all laugh together. So, of course, that was the first person I bumped into as I walked in. My nightmare was becoming reality.

We started chatting, and once we were done with the pleasantries, I explained the Plan, resigning myself to what would happen, but then I noticed something strange on Gordon's face. Something I did not expect to see there—genuine curiosity. He started peppering me with questions about the business and the Plan.

"How did you find this business?"

"It was actually through another friend from business school. I had relevant experience, and we both thought there was a great opportunity here."

"Is it hard leading such a large team?"

"So far, I have let the team continue with their current processes. I am still learning about the business and don't want to start changing things I still don't have a full grasp on."

"How are you learning about the industry?"

"Well, actually, I found the best way was to do each and every job in the company. So far, I've been a cashier in the store, attendant on the floor, receiver in the warehouse, and even a baker!"

"Oh wow, that's amazing! I know it's only been a few months, but what's been your biggest learning?"

"Honestly, I think you learn so much from doing all those jobs, but the key point is how interrelated all those functions are. If the warehouse doesn't open on time or sales are not uploaded properly in the system, it can impact the production of breads the next day. This interdependence is really fascinating."

While we were chatting, more people gathered around us.

No one laughed. Some found it strange, to be sure, but for the most part, and to my surprise (and relief), people loved the Plan. As I described it, I saw people around me who recognized this as a sound plan, some even wishing they had thought about this themselves. They wanted to hear more, going so far as letting me do the unthinkable in these reunions: take up more of their time and describe the three facets of the Plan in more detail.

Attending this reunion was a good idea after all.

Some of the friends I reconnected with helped with contacts in the industry and region. I even discovered some old friends I had lost touch with who now lived in neighboring countries (four-hour flights away, but that still counts). As I repeated the Plan again and again to more people, I was getting convinced. The Plan would work. By sweating the small stuff, I would learn the business better and succeed at it, then take that knowledge and become the best investor in the region.

I felt validated by my classmates' reactions, but it could have gone the other way. Would that have meant the Plan was wrong? Of course not. It would only have meant I had failed to properly explain it. In a way, the nervousness before the reunion helped me crystallize my case for the Plan.

> Lesson #2: Being nervous can help you crystallize your thoughts.

* * *

As I reflected on the reunion, I realized that before that moment, I only had to convince close friends and family about the soundness of the idea. I was nervous going to the reunion not so much for fear of being embarrassed but, rather, for fear of being caught with a poorly conceived plan. It would have been easy to poke holes in it. The reunion, coming so quickly after moving to Dar, was the chance for me to review the Plan in light of what I had learned those first months running Green Leaf. The Plan was always sound, but now it felt more tangible and there were fewer unknowns.

Truth be told, I still had doubts about the move. The first few months had not been easy. I was still getting the hang of the business, a lot of staff were reticent about working with me, and, with all the work, I couldn't find any time to discover and enjoy the country Neha and I had just moved to. I knew the entrepreneurial journey was a lonely one, but it dawned on me just how arduous it would be.

Many emerging market investors don't last or don't get the returns they expect. Why? Because they don't get their hands dirty. When you invest in an emerging market, you have to take the good—high growth, high margins—and the bad—difficult regulatory environment, lower levels of skills—and be ready to pull up your sleeves whenever you face any obstacles. You cannot be a suitcase investor; just dropping in with cash is not a competitive advantage. Your level of involvement in the business makes a difference, and I decided from the get-go to be all in, to face all the challenges, no matter what I knew or what they were.

Talking to peers and sharing what worked, what I hoped would work, and what I was unsure of felt like a relief. Although no one was doing the exact same thing I was, I could still find similarities in other people's work and lives, and it built up my confidence. It gave me a network I forgot I had, a support system I didn't think I needed and that would become critical in the coming years. After the reunion, I was ready to go back to Dar and take on the Green Leaf challenge with everything I had!

Little did I know at the time I'd need that confidence when I got back to Tanzania. Putting together a plan is one thing, but executing it is another story altogether...

Before we get to that, I suppose I still haven't answered the obvious question: How exactly did I end up buying this supermarket chain in Tanzania in the first place?

RAM'S TIPS:

- Sharing your goals can be daunting, but it doesn't have to be. Rehearse them, poke holes, share with a close group of family and friends first to test it out before broadcasting it to a larger audience. In the end, you will have to trust that it is the right thing for you.

- Being nervous is good because it can help you crystallize your thought process.

CHAPTER 3

THE HOOK

———

There you are, in a staid meeting room probably at your lawyer's office. You're about to sign those few pages that will entitle you to own a business, either by acquiring one or starting one yourself. All those years and months of anticipation for becoming an entrepreneur are coming to an end.

Congratulations, you've done it!

Or have you? Have you really thought this through? Before you sign those papers, imagine yourself five years from now. Were the sacrifices you made to get there worth it? How will you define success or failure?

What if you receive an email from someone who wants to buy your business? Are you ready to sell? What do they think it's worth? What do you think it's worth? If you sell, what will you do afterward?

It's critical to ask yourself these questions before you take on such a big commitment. Once the business is running, with employees and their families counting on you for their livelihood, customers needing your product, and loans from the bank, you can't back out. So before anything else, start by defining your vision and goals. Imagine yourself five years on; what would you like to see?

* * *

Let me rewind to the fall of 2015, when I found myself in New York. I had just gotten married and moved there while finalizing the sale of Kingdom Plaza and trying to figure out my next move.

Acquire more properties? In Houston or in the New York metro area?

Find a job? Was I tired of doing this all on my own?

I needed some time to reflect and decide on the best way forward when one of my closest friends from business school reached out. I met Nijhad even before starting school. Once you get accepted, Harvard connects you to other future students living in close proximity. Even among the dozens of high achievers I met that evening in New York, Nijhad stood out. First, because we looked similar, people confused us for brothers... except Nijhad is the skinnier one, with a beard and much better dressed.

What made our friendship last through the years is because of his capacity to listen and give honest feedback... even if that's not what you want to hear! He's one of the most thoughtful and intellectual people I know, who takes the time to understand the situation from all perspectives before giving his opinion. I appreciate that deeply.

Nijhad used to live in New York but had recently moved to London. He was back in the city for a few days, and I was eager to hear how he was doing.

We decided to try this new Scandinavian coffee shop around 50th Street and Lexington Avenue. Italy may come to mind first when you think of coffee, but Swedish people have an equal obsession with espresso! I got there first and marveled at the simplicity of the design. The color scheme was a simple black and white with a light wood accent for the counter and shelves, which displayed books about coffee, beans from all over the world, and an assortment of filters arranged neatly like a museum. Indeed, this place looked more like an ode to coffee than your typical coffee shop. Once Nijhad arrived, we ordered expertly made drinks and settled in a booth. After a few minutes catching up, he leaned forward and put his hands on the table, looking suddenly much more solemn.

"I'm not sure I told you before, but my family is originally from East Africa, and I've been spending more and more time in the region lately looking for a business to acquire," he said, letting the statement linger in the air for a few seconds.

"It took some time, but I found a business for sale that checks all the boxes. I wanted to chat with you about it. I think you'll love being involved."

I put down my coffee, intrigued. I was always up for helping a friend evaluate businesses. I had invested in startups before and advised a few people in starting their own company and raising money. I found this to be a great learning opportunity: you get to understand a different industry, what problems other businesses face and how people identify them, the paths they take to solve those problems, and how they manage to build and grow their business through it all. This often has many parallels with my own situation and helps me see issues in a new light or even before they arise.

"Involved how?" I asked.

"Well, it's a supermarket chain with four stores headquartered in Dar es Salaam, Tanzania called Green Leaf Supermarket. The family who started it still runs it, and they focus on selling high-quality food and drinks, most of which needs to be imported. They're one of the first chains in the country and have a first-mover advantage that way. Green Leaf is also at the forefront of the healthy/superfoods trend in the region and made a name for themselves in the category. Overall, they're like Whole Foods in the United States or Woolworths in South Africa, but with more logistics involved because of the imports. It's doing really well but could do even better."

"That's interesting indeed. So how can I help?"

"Well, the good news is it's been running for over twelve years now and there's a full team in place. The customer-facing part is great, with a strong emphasis on service. But the logistics and back-end operations are still run like a one-store family business with no proper systems or processes to track what is sold, what needs to be reordered, exact cost of goods, etc. I think there's a huge opportunity for you and me to partner and expand the concept throughout the region."

I was on my phone still trying to find Dar es Salaam on a map when I almost spit my coffee in shock.

"Wait, what do you mean partner? I'm happy to help and advise, but you want us to run it together? And move to... Tanzania? I don't even know where Dar es Salaam is on a map or the first thing about supermarkets!"

Nijhad put his hand up to stop me. He clearly knew this would be my response and had prepared his thoughts.

"Hear me out. First, there is a significant component of real estate in the business and choosing locations is everything in this. You have that experience.

"Two, you have general operational expertise from your past work, and while the markets are different, you have the right mindset for understanding the space and growing it. I can see from your work in Houston, you don't hesitate to get your hands dirty and do all the hard work. Combined with your international outlook and experience, this is exactly what Green Leaf needs! And as for the local context, you can learn it from the current management.

"Last, but not least, there's already a full team in place running the stores. We'd keep the same management, so yes, there's a learning curve on running a supermarket, but it's not like we're starting from scratch!"

I trusted Nijhad; he had been working in East Africa for the last few years and seen the opportunities available there firsthand. I had only been to South Africa and Kenya on consulting projects, but from what I saw during those trips and what I knew of Nijhad's work, I had no doubt that opportunities existed.

When you've worked and traveled enough, you realize there's potential and momentum almost everywhere. The trick is to identify the right trends and capitalize on them. Food retail in East Africa was one of those trends.

Still, there's a difference between visiting a place and moving there to run a business. I needed time to think about this and discuss it with my wife, Neha.

On the one hand, this sounded like an exciting opportunity. We'd acquire an existing business with an experienced team, sales, and cash flow. This wasn't the same as when I started looking for properties in Houston and had to learn everything on my own, unsure of whom to trust or even talk to.

On the other hand came the personal aspects. Were we ready to leave our families and friends in the United States behind?

It was a lot to absorb. Was it a little exciting? Yes. Did it sound like a challenge? Yes, but in the beginning, I was worried it was too outlandish and dismissed the idea to Neha outright.

"So, how was your coffee with Nijhad?" she asked when I came home later that day.

"It was nice. He's adjusting to life in London and enjoying his move there. And guess what, he wants us to move to Africa and for me to run a supermarket chain there! Can you believe it?"

I thought Neha would join in my laughter, but instead, she perked up.

"Where in Africa? And what do you mean run a supermarket chain?"

I gave her the full background and a strong caveat that I didn't think it was a good idea.

"Why?" She asked.

"Well, because our lives are here. And what do I know about running supermarkets?"

"Think about the number of times you told me that you thought you knew real estate and yet your Houston experience was miles away from anything you ever learned at school or in your previous work. You don't think you could learn this too? Could be interesting..."

"Yes, but it's in Tanzania. I mean, do you really want to move to Dar es Salaam? What would you do there? And we'd be so far away from everyone we know. Are we even able to make new friends?"

"We discussed that we'd love to live somewhere else for a few years. I'm sure I'll find work, and we're not such horrible people that we couldn't make new friends!"

Neha didn't let up. She grew up moving and living in different countries, so this was not out of her comfort zone.

"Besides, you said you're feeling in a rut these days while trying to figure out your next move. Frankly, I don't think you enjoy working in the United States as much as you say.

The market and system are almost too rigid for you. You need someplace where the opportunities are bare, and you'll thrive on figuring those things out. I know that much about you."

She wasn't far off the mark. At this point in my career, I had worked in the United States and India predominantly, and I enjoyed India far more. To succeed in the United States, I felt like you needed a great new idea or to invent the next best thing. In India, you needed a relentless focus on execution, doing the same things repeatedly until obstacles are surmounted or bypassed. I was better at the latter but was stuck in trying to do the former.

It was something to mull over. Over the following weeks, Nijhad sent me more information about the business opportunities in the country and the region, and his vision for what Green Leaf could become.

When I started evaluating this move in terms of my professional goals, my perspective on the opportunity shifted. After all, I was saying I needed to do all the small things in business, sweat the small stuff, and get an intuition for how a company works and grows. This was that chance—to run and grow my own company; operate in a complicated but high-growth emerging market; go through the process of acquisition and operations; and eventually exit. I could use the core business principles I learned from business school, combine them with my practical knowledge working in other similar markets, and make the operational improvements and innovations necessary to manage and grow the business.

This seemed like a good plan to improve my business skills and become a better investor, a theme I'd talked about ever since that dinner in India.

On the personal side, Neha and I had discussed moving from New York and living somewhere else. We didn't know exactly where or for what, but it was part of our goals for our life together.

Neha was right, perhaps there was something here for me.

Investment Criteria #1: Does it match your personal and professional goals?

Answer: Yes!

Before agreeing to anything, I had to see the opportunity firsthand.

* * *

I landed in Dar es Salaam in the middle of November. It had been unusually cold in New York, but the tropical heat of Dar hit me like a turkey roasting in the oven.

First impressions were muted. The airport looked like it was built in the sixties (turns out, it was), smaller even than most regional airports found elsewhere. The outside was grey cement built in what I can only describe as a brutalist style, reminiscent of some parts of Moscow, where buildings are designed for functionality and not to be pleasing to the eye.

Inside was not much better—no air conditioning, throngs of people pushing and pulling through the immigration queue, walls painted a strange yellow that was peeling off, and signs either hastily handwritten or printed on A4 paper. Not exactly reassuring in terms of progress.

I had flown in with Nijhad. As soon as we stepped out of the terminal, we were greeted by Amir, the owner of the supermarket chain, and his family. Their warm welcome was amplified by the surrounding heat.

As we pulled out of the brutalist-styled airport, they pointed out the new airport under construction. Now that building was something to look at! It was a shining amalgamation of steel and glass, almost completely see-through, and could rival newer airports found in India or China. Things were perking up.

We had to drive through the center of town to get to the hotel. It was a Sunday and things were slow, but you could still feel a certain energy in the air. At every red light, throngs of young people were walking by selling car accessories, newspapers, snacks, cool drinks, books, even large maps of Tanzania! You feel a similar energy in other markets that are starting to open up and embrace a form of capitalism—optimism for the future if you can work hard enough.

I slept that night with a mix of emotions. Moving from the United States to a country as low in the economic rankings as Tanzania felt like a step back, but I also knew deep down that the unbound energy could be a great source of growth.

The next day, we visited the main and largest store of Green Leaf Supermarket. I had seen photos posted by customers on Google, and the business had an infrequently updated Facebook page, but the real thing was different.

The driver dropped us off in front of the store, and we walked in through a large double sliding door entrance. The first thing I noticed was how clean everything looked. No shelves were messy with items out of place, all products had a proper price tag neatly stuck below it, trolleys and baskets were free of detritus. There was even a notice board for anyone to post about events or items for sale that seemed like an Instagram collage of flyers.

The second thing I noticed was how bright things were. The lighting was a cool white and covered every inch of the store—not so harsh that you need to squint, but not so dim that you need a flashlight for reading product labels. The bright lights also added to the sense of cleanliness.

The third thing I noticed was the smiles of the staff. The moment I entered, I was greeted by a warm smile and heartfelt "Karibu," which I quickly learned means "welcome" and so many other things in Swahili.

I was getting that Whole Foods feeling.

My apprehensions about taking over what I thought was a mom-and-pop operation quickly vanished as I walked through the aisles and saw the care and order with which goods were placed on the shelves. Everything was labeled and priced correctly, shelves were organized by category, and you could find everything you wanted there.

I was not sure yet if prices were competitive, but I sure felt welcomed and comfortable about shopping in this environment. They had successfully created a modern, organized supermarket, selling a blend of local and international products, all wrapped with a definite sense of Tanzanian warmth.

> **Investment Criteria #2: Do you get a good, positive feeling in your gut about the investment?**

Answer: Yes!

I had to check one more thing before ending this trip: how much money did this business actually make?

* * *

Green Leaf started as a one-store operation but grew in the last few years to four stores. They kept good records of daily sales at each store, but tracking expenses was a bit trickier.

No centralized system was in place to understand supplier payments, payroll, or other administrative expenses. There were audited financials of course, but they lumped many expenses together and did not give clear enough insight into the business. Instead, they used a collection of Excel spreadsheets and accounting software from the dinosaur age to enter lump-sum payments manually.

Of all things to come to mind at that point, I remembered from my Technology & Operations Management class to "follow the product" when you wanted to know how a supply chain really worked. In this case, if I wanted to answer the profitability question, perhaps I could follow the cash from the moment it entered the tills until it left the company bank accounts.

I knew sales were coming in; that much was clear. Whether I visited the stores on a Saturday at 11:00 a.m. during prime hours or on Tuesday afternoons when it's supposed to be quiet, there were always shoppers.

I also knew expenses needed to be covered. Landlords, suppliers, staff—all those bills needed to be paid monthly.

The answer was to look at what happened to the excess cash, if there was any. If the business was profitable, cash would be paid to the owners, hopefully year after year. If the business was not profitable, the owners would not pay themselves, which wouldn't be a good sign.

It took me some time to go through all the company's bank statements. Being an importer, the company had accounts not only in Tanzanian Shillings but also US Dollars, British Pounds, and Euros. To sift through all the payments moving from account to account was not easy, but eventually, I found what I was looking for. Once a year, between February and April, payment was sent from the company to a different account, which I learned belonged to the owners.

The amount varied from year to year, but it represented between 6 and 10 percent of annual sales. From the little I knew about profitability in retail, this seemed exceptional.

> **Investment Criteria #3: Is the business profitable?**

Answer: Yes!

They were a smart, entrepreneurial family, and I could see that even though they didn't know complicated financial lingo, they understood cash. Cash is not always the best metric to use because it doesn't cover things like debt or suppliers that have invoices outstanding, but the business had been running like this for twelve years. If there were any deeper issues with the bank or suppliers, that would have come out by now.

Between the audited financials and the bank statements, we had a decent handle on Green Leaf's cash flows.

We finished our due diligence with visits to the competitors to understand the market in more detail. The difference was stark—no service or even warm smile upon entering, not nearly as big a selection, and a store design that could only rival the drab airport we'd arrived in. On the basic products, however, like milk and sugar, their prices were 3 to 5 percent cheaper than Green Leaf. They were playing the price game and sacrificed everything else in their quest to push volume.

Yet sales at Green Leaf were growing well in the last few years. This was a clear indication the market was growing and there was room for us and the competition. More importantly, sales of the specialty products (think gluten, dairy, or sugar-free) were growing at an even faster pace and were nowhere to be found in the competing supermarkets. Green Leaf was playing in its own niche and doing well.

> **Investment Criteria #4: Did you find anything concerning with the business or market during due diligence? Any trends that seem to indicate people are buying less of the product?**

Answer: No!

Using the cash figure we found above would also help value the business and put a price forward. I went back to New York and had more discussions with my soon-to-be partner. We agreed on a price along with a few conditions that needed to be met. Now that we had both seen the business and finished the due diligence, we could come up with our initial vision for Green Leaf. We put together a financial forecast, investment thesis, what we saw as the growth opportunities, and a five-year growth plan that helped us think through how we would make money from this purchase.

We came up with an agreement on a single piece of paper. If everyone trusted each other, that's all it took. If there was no trust, it didn't matter whether you had one page or one hundred, the agreement would not work.

> **Investment Criteria #5: Taking into account all the risks identified during due diligence, can you buy the business at a reasonable price?**

Answer: Yes!

> **Investment Criteria #5A: Are you sure you're not getting carried away by your emotions? Remember what happened in Houston!**

Answer: No, I am not. I learned my lesson, and this works!

And there we had it. We had acquired the business from Amir. We worked out a plan for him to transition slowly out of the business while we learned the ropes.

I still think Amir was surprised I moved from New York to Dar es Salaam. Most people go the other way around in search of an opportunity, but there I was, on March 2, 2016, less than six months after my first meeting with Nijhad, showing up at the airport in Dar again, this time ready to run the business.

This was home now. I was determined to make it work, come what may.

RAM'S TIPS:
How do you know you're making a good investment?

- It has to get you excited.

- It should match your personal and professional goals.

- You have to have a positive gut feel about it.

- It has to make money!

- Diligence it thoroughly. It is especially reassuring when your customers (no matter how few they are today) love the product. This will form the backbone of your vision for the business.

- Make sure to buy it at a reasonable price, without getting carried away by your emotions.

CHAPTER 4

PARTNERSHIP IS AN ART

"Just let me do it, I will be faster."

"No, let's think about it first. We're missing something," replied Nijhad.

We were having an intense discussion about costs and margins. We knew, overall, the business had approximately 30 percent gross margin, but when we analyzed the financials store by store or category by category, we were nowhere close. It was impossible to reconcile.

"Look again at the calculation of our product costing vs. the retail price, I think we're double-counting the value-added tax," I said.

"We need to look at the bigger picture. We know how much we're paying our suppliers, and we can check if that matches the total cost of products we get from them."

It was even harder to reconcile our working styles. I like to constantly be moving and doing multiple things together—thinking came while I was doing something else.

Nijhad liked to take his time through each task, going step by step to make sure we didn't make a mistake. For him, there was no point in doing anything further if we got some assumptions wrong.

In other words, I had a bias toward "doing" and he, toward "thinking."

One isn't better than the other, but whenever we were both working on a problem together, whether at school or during the Green Leaf years, we butted heads. I wanted to "do" and he wanted to "think." Ultimately, that combination is why we became friends and successful business partners. Our styles were complementary, and we pushed each other. You often hear the saying "don't get into business with your friend." I find that strange. If you can't trust your friend to start a company, then will you really trust a stranger? Business is a marriage, and if I'm going to marry someone, I'd rather know the good—keeps calm under pressure, no emotional highs or lows—and the not-so-good—does not always share the full plan before it is perfect, can be overwhelmed by bad news. Having a personal experience rather than seeing it firsthand when we're dealing with a crisis is best.

At the same time, it's important to establish upfront roles and responsibilities, boundaries, what we enjoy doing, and what we won't tolerate. Before getting married, Neha and I spent a lot of time discussing our values, goals, hopes, and dreams. It's strange to say, but Nijhad and I did something similar.

* * *

Before finalizing the acquisition, we spent time together discussing every possible scenario we could think of and how each of us would deal with it.

"What if I need to fire a senior manager and you're not reachable?"

"What if our container is stuck at port because of an unscrupulous official?"

"What if I caught a staff member stealing?"

"What if one of our employees asked me for a loan?"

"What if the bank calls and refuses to renew our loans?" No scenario was too big or too small to discuss. Even in matters of personal relationships, it's important to sweat the small stuff.

Of course, when you're in the thick of things and managing crisis after crisis, it's hard to remember what was agreed and who was supposed to do what. So let me outline what I believe worked for us and what didn't work as well that had to be course-corrected.

First, it is critical to always keep communication lines open. In the early days especially, we were on the phone every day. Whether it's good or bad news, you think you know how your friend will react, but being business partners brings out different sides of your personality. It's easy to take for granted that they will accept whatever decision you make. It's better to communicate more than less. At worst, you spent a few minutes on the phone catching up. In the best case, you might get great insight or a different point of view on something that was nagging.

Second, it is critical to establish clear roles and responsibilities from the beginning. For any tasks or projects assigned to either partner, figure out deadlines and milestones to keep each other on top of things and accountable. This will also ensure that everyone else in the company knows who to go to for any specific problem they face. Don't make any assumptions. If in doubt, write it out.

Upfront, we decided Nijhad would stay in London and come to Dar regularly to advance his tasks. His role revolved around finance and strategy. I would be the person on the ground managing operations.

Having agreed to that, I had expected Nijhad and I to spend the first three months on the ground together. He understood our agreement to be valid immediately and had other obligations in London. Two weeks after arriving in this new country and city to run this business I knew nothing about, Nijhad left and I felt I was alone.

He thought he had been clear, which led to a few messy conversations early on about who was more dedicated to the business.

"Why did you leave Dar so quickly? I thought we were going to figure this out together?"

"Sorry, Ram, I had to be in London this weekend. There's a wedding in the family, and I had to be there for it."

"Good for you. In the meantime, I am left all alone here to do the work. I really thought we were in this together."

"Of course we are! Look, I am sorry I didn't tell you about this. I thought our agreement was clear from the beginning. I'll come back to Dar on Monday first thing."

We both learned an important lesson. Don't make assumptions about what the other person is thinking or their commitment level.

Here's another example of clearly establishing boundaries. Finance & Accounting was solely Nijhad's remit. Whenever Balendra had a question, he liked to come to my office to discuss it. I didn't mind those conversations, but I was clear from the beginning that he needed to be in touch with Nijhad and that picking up the phone should be as comfortable as walking over to my office. After all, I was often on the move visiting stores and suppliers, so he couldn't expect to just wait for someone to show up before making a decision.

This also removed a lot of unnecessary stress. Knowing that he was looking after Finance helped me focus on understanding the operations. And knowing I was on top of our ordering meant Nijhad wasn't stressed about that.

Third, write out your goals and align your vision for the next five years. At the end of our first visit to Dar, we spent time discussing what each of us envisioned for the business.

- Where could it go?

- How could we make it better?

- What would be the exciting parts of the journey and what would be the difficult ones?

- How would we handle those?

These questions led us to discuss why we were even buying this business in the first place and opening up more about our respective backgrounds and choices.

For Nijhad, it was family pride. He was originally from East Africa and growing businesses in the region was a way of giving back to a community that had given his family so much.

For me, it was a way to learn managerial skills and get a better intuition for business. And personally, Neha and I wanted to live in a new part of the world. I could kill two birds with one stone.

Fourth, be open with each other. We each made many mistakes along the way—some small and some not so small—but we were always transparent about what happened and figured out a way to move forward together. The needs of the business came first, and we both understood that. Personal feelings mattered less when we were days away from running out of cash and needed to think creatively and quickly about a solution. We left the post-mortem of what went wrong for after the crisis and never played the blame game. At some point, it all evens out anyway!

Finally, make time to be friends. Nijhad and I went through great pains to be professional at the office and in the stores, only focusing on work-talk, but when it was just the two of us or we were with our spouses out for dinner, we actively spent time discussing things other than Green Leaf. Even when we traveled to Nairobi to set up the store there, we became roommates in a small, rented apartment. We made an effort to talk about what was going on in our lives, like we used to before the supermarket days.

A partnership built on mutual respect, trust, and communication can be hugely successful and turn around any situation. We saw it many times over the next four years growing Green Leaf, but it is important to remember it is a living, breathing thing that needs to be worked on every day and never taken for granted.

As for the issues with margins, we managed to find out the answer. Turns out we did have an issue in accounting for the value-added tax, but our suppliers also gave us volume discounts at the end of each month, and those weren't taken into account in the system's product costing. Combining both our insights led us to figure it out!

RAM'S TIPS:

- Five steps to set up an effective partnership:

  - Communicate at all times

  - Establish clear roles and responsibilities

  - Write out your goals and align your vision

  - Be open with each other

  - Make time to be friends

CHAPTER 5

THROUGH A
RABBIT HOLE

If you're like me, you've probably shopped a thousand times in
a supermarket and never really thought about how they made
money. Sure, you might hear that big chains like Walmart or Car-
refour have razor-thin profit margins, but considering how many
times you go shopping, have you ever stopped and wondered
why? And why do they keep running out of that special product
you love so much? Whenever you find it, you must stock three
times more than you actually need. Feels annoying, doesn't it?

I certainly hadn't thought deeply about any of those issues,
but it was time to find out the nuts and bolts of this operation,
but where to start?

* * *

We had four stores, a head office, and a warehouse. One morning I was passing by the office when I heard a commotion
inside the Accounts department. A supplier there had come
to collect his payment, and he was visibly annoyed.

I took Balendra, our Head of Finance & Accounts, out of earshot of the supplier and asked him what was going on. Balendra was short and stocky, with a laugh that could carry across a room. He also had a mustache he took particular pride in grooming. At that moment though, neither he nor his mustache looked particularly happy.

"This is Mr. Vishal, one of our main suppliers. He says he supplied us with tomato cans on the condition that he would be paid within seven days, but we in Accounts were not aware and his check is not ready, so he is annoyed."

"Oh really? Why weren't you made aware?"

"Actually, you see, Procurement makes the orders, and we prepare the cheques after thirty days, so how are we supposed to know to pay him so quickly?"

"And you can't prepare a cheque for him now?"

"No, we don't even have the invoice yet from the warehouse, so on what basis can we prepare a cheque? And you know, Mr. Ram, this is an important supplier; this looks very bad on us."

I was miffed. I had been here less than a week and not versed enough in how things were done to know if this was standard practice or an exception to an otherwise well-oiled machine. From the way Balendra was speaking, I feared it might be the former.

I was also confused about why a can of tomatoes was ordered with such urgency that a supplier could command payment in one-fourth the normal time. Even I knew that canned goods had a long shelf life. This seems like a product we should have aplenty and allow us the full thirty days to pay the supplier.

I had to talk to our Procurement Manager, Kabir, to understand this better. He was in the warehouse, which was a ten-minute drive away. I didn't yet have a car, so had to wait for the company van to fetch me. It was used to bring employees early in the morning in different shifts, depending on what time they started, and then take them home in the evening. Instead of waiting in the hot Dar sun, I took refuge inside our air-conditioned store attached to the head office. This was the first store ever opened and was small but had a cozy, warm feeling—the same feeling I got from the more modern store I had visited the first time around.

I walked over to the canned goods section and saw a customer in deep thought holding two different cans. I was squinting trying to look at what he was holding when he noticed me. I must have looked so creepy watching over him like that, and I could see from his face he was a bit freaked out. He put both cans into his trolley and quickly walked away.

Strange behavior, I thought.

I walked over to the section to examine it in more detail. I still couldn't tell which cans he took, but I was not impressed by what I saw. The shelf was nearly empty. The only supplier I knew that sold tomato cans (at that point, really the *only* supplier I knew) was angry with us and didn't seem in the mood to supply us more.

I headed to the branch manager's office and asked Jeremy what was going on with the canned tomatoes.

"Big problem, sir. We keep ordering them from the warehouse, but they never send us enough."

We walked back to the canned foods section.

"Look at this, sir; it's pathetic. How are we supposed to make any sales if we don't have anything to sell? You have to do something about it!"

I was flattered Jeremy thought I could solve his problems, but I barely knew what the problem was myself. I never even bought canned tomatoes. Before moving to Dar, instead of using our tiny New York kitchen, we either ordered from restaurants or ate out.

> *Note to Self #1:*
>
> *I should cook more at home. It is healthier and will also help me keep track of what we sell and run out of in the store.*

As Jeremy kept describing all the varieties of canned tomatoes he was missing—diced, chopped, whole peeled, puree, chopped and peeled, chopped peeled and mixed with onions—I now understood what that customer I stalked was doing.

He must have been looking for a specific kind of can we didn't have and picked up the two that looked closest to what he was looking for. Confusing me for another customer, he probably panicked and bought both cans, worried that the store would run out!

Jeremy and I had a brief laugh about it, but we had to return to the serious business of finding more canned tomatoes. Now was the right time to put to good use what I remembered from my Operations class: follow the product.

* * *

We picked up the price sticker from the shelf (I didn't even know those came out!) and walked over to Amina, the store's Receiving Manager, at the back of the store. She was in charge of accepting products received from our warehouse or suppliers.

Amina scanned the barcode in her system, and we looked at the last date it was received. We could see dozens of pending orders for this product dating back weeks, but it was received only once, two days ago, and it was already running out. Twenty-four cans, or as they say in the industry, one case, was received for chopped, diced, and whole peeled tomatoes, when at least three more types were ordered. All these names were confusing, but it was clear no orders were getting fulfilled.

Worse, I knew from having just walked over from the shelf that we had run out of most of them. Were we really waiting until products were sold out to reorder them?

I turned to Jeremy and Amina.

"Why didn't you order more cans already?" I asked. "You received some of them the other day, so clearly there could be more stock at the warehouse."

Jeremy turned to Amina.

"Why didn't you order any of these? You know it's fast-moving, and now we won't have anything on the shelf for at least two days until the next warehouse delivery!"

Amina turned to the Shelf Attendant responsible for the canned goods section, who happened to walk by with his shelf stickers when he saw us huddling around the computer.

"Why didn't you tell me you needed more of these products? We should have placed an order days ago when you knew we were going to run out!"

The Shelf Attendant replied, "Actually, I told Jeremy a few days ago we were running out, but it was in the evening when he was closing the shop, so he must have forgotten."

This would've been funny if it wasn't so alarming. Jeremy was the only one authorized to place orders. Amina had to wait for his approval before sending out orders to the warehouse or suppliers. The process was set this way so there wouldn't be any over-ordering of products and no abuse by over-zealous attendants, but clearly, we now had the opposite problem and had run out of a critical item.

> **Possible Improvement #1:**
>
> How can we empower the Shelf Attendant to place an order? And couldn't the Receiving Manager check if something was needed based on past sales? This could be a way to bypass the overwhelmed Jeremy and ensure the shelves are full.

> *Note to Self #2:*
>
> *Those promotion flyers the Receiving Manager is printing has some typos. I know English isn't everyone's first language, but I also don't want to micromanage each piece of paper printed in the store. I have to find a way to help the team. It's not necessary to drive sales and wouldn't settle my current problem, but it would definitely help improve the store's image.*

I took note of the various tomato barcodes, hopped in the van, and headed to the warehouse. Samir, the Warehouse Manager, greeted me with a firm handshake and a big smile. He was excited to show me around and explain how his department worked.

I showed him the barcodes. He looked them up in his system and found that, indeed, he received an order ten days prior. He had been busy with a backlog for two days, but on the third day, tasked his team to put together the shipment for all the branches and send out all the goods they had. Each store wanted to get five cases at least, but he only managed to send two per store.

> **Possible Improvement #2:**
>
> **If we're running out of products, this means lost sales. If I can figure out how to stop us from selling out of products, this will be an easy way to increase sales.**

"Why can't we fulfill the orders placed by the stores?" I asked Samir.

"That is all that was left in stock, so we sent them everything we had," he responded.

"Why didn't you just order more from the supplier then?"

"I don't place those orders. Kabir, the Procurement Manager does. Please ask him."

So, along with my barcodes, I went to find Kabir. He was inside a small-ish office he shared with Sandra, the Pricing Manager.

> *Note to Self #3:*
>
> *Another manager? We might have an issue with title inflation. If everyone is a manager, then where is the scope for promotion? And if we can't use titles to emphasize a promotion, how do we motivate people?*

Kabir scanned the barcodes and realized we had no stock in the warehouse or in any of our stores. We had run out after sending the last batch a few days ago. I asked him why he wasn't made aware we had sold out.

Now it turns out he was not informed it had run out at the warehouse. Although he was sitting in an office located inside it, the place was big and messy, with thousands of products spread out. When the staff is busy or overwhelmed, they forget to inform him.

Kabir also missed it because there was no easy way for him to know what would either sell out or was already sold out.

"Wait," I said. "In front of us is software that tracks all the products received and sent? You're looking at it now and it shows we're sold out... so why don't you use the software?"

"We have not cleaned up the product database since the company started. There are over 55,000 products on here, half of which we probably don't sell anymore, so if I pull up a list of products that are sold out, it's going to be long... very long sir."

> *Note to self #4:*
>
> *Talk to IT about cleaning up the database to make our operations more efficient and the team more productive.*

"Also, sir, the categories are incorrect. See, this can of tomatoes is saved in the Toiletries category, but it should be under Grocery."

Duh, that's obvious, I thought.

> *Expanded Note to Self #4:*
>
> *Urgently talk to IT about cleaning up the database, including checking all categories.*

"Ok, so now you know the product is sold out. What are you going to do about it?"

"I will see how we can order it."

"Could you do it now, please?" I said. "I am curious to see how the ordering system works."

I thought this was an innocent question and the answer should have been straightforward, but I was about to come face to face with my first big cultural challenge. Kabir started fumbling with his keyboard, looking for the product on the system, scanning the barcodes again and again, but somehow getting nowhere. After a good fifteen minutes of watching him do effectively nothing on the screen, I had to say something.

"What's the problem? Is the computer not working?"

"No, sir, actually with this particular product, it is difficult to order it."

"Why?"

"Because, sir, actually this product we normally order it from abroad. And so when we run out, we can only get a few varieties from a local supplier if he has it."

"Ok, so unless the supplier has run out, why don't we order whatever varieties he has until our next import?"

"Because, sir, the local supplier is not happy with us."

"Yes, I know, I met him earlier and he was furious because his payment was not ready. Balendra told me he was not aware that he had to pay them on such short notice. Do you know what that's about?"

"Because, sir..."

Kabir started mumbling something and I couldn't quite understand what he was trying to say. This game of cat-and-mouse (or should I say "why-and-because, sir") was getting tedious, but I kept following up without betraying any sense of frustration.

I later learned that Tanzanians are averse to giving bad news, and that's why Kabir was so hesitant to share the real issue with me. Everyone here feels that the bearer of bad news is the one who will get shot. This was the flip side of everyone being so warm, it was happening almost to a fault!

As a result, there wasn't a strong culture of objectively identifying the issues and working together to fix them.

Finally, after a bit of pushing and prodding, the answer came out.

"Because, sir, Balendra knows, but Mr. Amir doesn't like paying suppliers that early. We try to manage it, but it's not easy. And this product, sir, we really need it, so I had to order it."

There it was, the crux of this issue. The way I saw it, we didn't import enough in the first place because our system could not accurately and in a timely manner tell us, among the thousands of products we import, how much we should buy and how quickly we would run out of items. After all, if we were selling half a dozen types of just canned tomatoes, imagine how many product variations we had to sort through!

All this snowballed into trying to order from a local supplier who not only charges us more but doesn't give us much time to pay. Bottom line: fewer sales, more cost.

> **Possible Improvement #3:**
>
> **Find out how the system can better track sales and stock-outs. If we can order better based on historical sales data, we won't miss out on lost sales and try to compensate by buying more expensively from another supplier. More sales, less cost!**

I felt satisfied to find three possible improvements in just one day. I didn't want to rush into implementing anything just yet though. I had barely scratched the surface of how the stores operated and needed more time watching and learning.

A good side benefit: the senior team saw me as someone willing to come to them to understand their work rather than the usual managers, who stayed in their office. This would be useful to gain their confidence.

Nevertheless, this confirmed Nijhad's and my initial analysis, that the back operations needed work. And you thought it was easy to make money running a supermarket!

RAM'S TIPS:

- In the beginning, just ask, watch, and learn. If people want your opinion or a decision from you, resist the urge.

- When identifying problems, think about the root cause.

- When identifying solutions, consider whether that fix is scalable.

CHAPTER 6

DRESS FOR SUCCESS

So many things to learn and so many things to do. My days started earlier and earlier. While I wanted to spend as much time as possible inside the stores, it also took a lot of effort to go through our database to understand the data. Yet the more time I spent on it, the less I felt like I was accomplishing anything.

The issue wasn't the availability of data. Every item sold each day was recorded down to the second it was scanned at the till. The issue was quality. The problems identified through the can of tomatoes episode were widespread, and thousands of items were miscategorized, misnamed, or, worst of all, duplicated.

Why is that bad, you ask? Because of a report I discovered in our system that was supposed to be helpful but turned out to be a nightmare. This was the "Sales vs. Purchase" report.

As its name implies, it's supposed to compare what we purchased to what we sold in a given time period. So you could say, "Look at how many cans of soda we bought that month and see how many we sold." Some months we sold everything, which means we're losing on sales, or some months we had a balance of stock left, which meant we were potentially overbuying.

You could even run that report by supplier to see the sales performance of each of them and their products. The issue was that somehow different codes had been used to record a product entering the system and the barcodes used for selling them. It was complete chaos. For many of our suppliers, it would show purchases against which there were no sales!

I knew that wasn't true, but how could I sort out the real data from all this?

I couldn't escape what I had to do next: clean up the database with products we actually sold, fix the miscategorizations, and combine the duplicates. This was not a fun task. Just downloading our product list took over ten minutes; it was fifty thousand items long!

I wouldn't let this deter me. This was my first step in cleaning up our operations, and I would get this right.

Kondo, our Information Technology (IT) Manager, was excited about this task. He had been trying to get everyone at Green Leaf to buy into the system more and use it judiciously. It's always a chicken-and-egg problem with databases: you have to use it well first before you see how easy it can make your life, but if you don't do it from the beginning, you risk having garbage data and then never seeing its value. That's what happened here, and now everything was in a rut.

We didn't have any extra resources to help, so I used the website Upwork, to find a few people to help sort out the data. I sent them part of the file with clear instructions and then checked what they did. It worked out efficiently, and we managed to get through the entire data set in five weeks.

Between the items we hadn't sold in years and the duplicates, we reduced the number of SKUs (Stock Keeping Units, the number of products we sold in the store) by over half! As a side benefit, this also meant our servers would run faster and smoother.

I was probably more excited than one should be looking at a datasheet of supermarket products, but this was the first real thing I had accomplished at Green Leaf, and I felt proud. Besides Kondo, no one else in the company really got why it was so important to have a clean database.

But no matter! I was convinced we could do so much with the data. My episode with the tomato cans proved that with the right information, we could sell more, save more, and free everyone's time. Now I just had to convince others to start following me on this journey.

* * *

How do you get a team of over 150 people behind you? Even if you could call a meeting with everyone present (and I couldn't because the stores were open seven days a week for twelve hours a day), what do you say? I needed a way to rally everyone around a common goal. An Excel spreadsheet wouldn't be it.

Lesson #1: Know your company history.

That's when I remembered an important lesson from my marketing classes at Harvard. For a business to build its future, it must know its heritage. And once it knows where it came from, it can focus on where it is going. How does it do that? By articulating a clear vision and mission statement.

The mission statement is a short sentence or paragraph of why an organization exists, what its overall goal is, what kind of product or service it provides, its primary customers or market, and its geographical region of operation. The vision declares the company's objectives, intended to guide everyone's decision-making.

At Green Leaf, we had none of those explicitly written out and shared with all employees, so that was the first order of business.

What were we about exactly? Nijhad and I had gone through a long exercise to figure out where we wanted to be five years from now, but how could we connect that to Green Leaf's heritage?

The simplest was to start from the beginning and speak to Amir, who had created the business twelve years ago. His thesis was fascinatingly simple. There was only one other formal supermarket in the *country* at that time, and they didn't have many products (there were, of course, informal markets). He had another business importing electronics from Dubai, so he thought, why not bring a few food items and see how they sell. It was a hit!

People were craving different foods and, to his credit, many items he brought were not even available in Tanzania at the time. He was also at the forefront of the healthy food movement and was the first to stock superfoods like quinoa or goji berries on the shelves.

I now had a sense of our history but needed to understand what Green Leaf represented for the community, both our customers and employees.

> **Lesson #2: To understand how others perceive your company, speak to all stakeholders: customers, staff, and suppliers. It will help you understand why they interact with you.**

I embarked on a multi-week, multi-store journey to speak to some of our oldest staff who had been there from the very beginning to some of the more recent hires. Along the way, I also spoke with customers, some who had been shopping with us since we opened and others who had just discovered us. The answers were insightful. The oldest staff talked about the quality and variety of our products. Our oldest customers echoed the point about variety and focused on our quality. They knew we sold good products and could always count on us to find what they needed.

Our newer employees were more interested in our reputation as a good place to work and our service. They liked talking to customers and helping them find our cutting-edge products.

The customers who had just discovered us did so often because they were looking for healthy or diet-specific products. They might have been intolerant to wheat and looking for gluten-free breads, or allergic to dairy and wanted to get soy or almond milk, or just on a diet and switched to brown pasta. Whatever the case, they could find those products in our stores.

After spending probably dozens of hours speaking to customers and our staff in all our stores, and understanding why people shopped here instead of the competition, it dawned on me how we could express Green Leaf's mission.

We were not about providing the best price. I knew from the way we sourced our products, the quality of those products, and our rents in various locations that we could not beat others on price. No one even mentioned it in my conversations.

I also knew we were not a warehouse-type store that leaves goods on pallets for customers to shop. We had organized shelves with proper lighting and good service.

We were a store that stocked high-quality products from all over the world and whose staff prided itself on helping our customers.

After writing it out, I realized our mission statement was simple: to offer our customers the best possible product and service in a welcoming, friendly, and fun shopping environment. Our vision derived from the research we performed in those months before acquiring the business, and the potential we saw to become the premier supermarket in East Africa, serving customers looking for a unique selection of products combined with the best in-store experience and customer service.

If these sentences sound corny and overly simple, it's because they are meant to be. They are created that way to help anyone within the company make the right choice when facing a problem.

Here is an example of one such situation faced by a store manager.

One Saturday afternoon, a customer in our Peninsula branch inquired about buying a red velvet cake mix to make for her daughter that weekend, but the store had run out. She asked Ali, the branch manager, who checked the other stores and learned we had stock in our Bongoyo branch. However, the customer did not have time to go across town to buy this item. Disappointment was written all over the mother and daughter's face.

Our mission is to offer the best service, so what did our manager do? He called the other branch and asked them to immediately send over some stock of red velvet cake mix by taxi. Within thirty minutes, the customer got her cake mix and left happy.

This did not bode well for our margins, but our mission was not simply to be the most profitable. Our mission was to have the best products and the best service, and we believed this would be the key to building customer loyalty. Customer loyalty eventually would translate into profits.

That same customer regularly shopped at our store over the years I spent in Dar, and she frequently recounted to others the story of how Green Leaf rushed a taxi from the other side of town so she could go home and bake her daughter her favorite cake.

You can't buy that kind of love.

* * *

All that was good and well, but how would we communicate this to the staff and the outside world. We needed a way to show our mission statement to the world.

Like many of my early ideas, this one came from the employees. While I was visiting one of the stores and asking the staff what they were doing and how they were doing it, someone approached me and sheepishly asked to speak to me in private.

We went to the side of the store to talk.

"Sir, I have a request, please," he said.

"Yes, tell me," I answered.

"Well, I am grateful for the job here at Green Leaf; it makes me very proud. I am happy with the salary, and you even pay me for transport, so thank you, sir. The problem is I don't have that much money left after I cover my expenses. And I don't have proper clothes to wear to come to work. I was told to find a white shirt and black pants, but this shirt is old, and I feel it doesn't give a good image to the company. Why don't we have uniforms, sir?"

Wow, uniforms! I couldn't believe I hadn't realized none of the staff were wearing uniforms! They all were wearing the same color scheme, but there was no logo, nothing to show they were part of Green Leaf. And no name tags either.

We couldn't be about quality and service if our staff was not wearing clothes they could be proud of. This would be the first order of business, the first cheque I would sign: uniforms for all the staff.

Within two weeks, we found a local seamstress with quality fabric. She went to all our stores and took everyone's measurements—two sets of clothing for every staff and a name tag. The shirt had our logo emblazoned on the front above the side pocket. On the back, written in a semi-circle across the top, was our new motto: Quality, Variety, Service.

As we were about to receive the uniforms, I panicked. What if that employee was just a bit disgruntled and uniforms did not matter? What if people did not like wearing uniforms? I was not a fan, so how could I assume everyone would fall in line and wear it? After all, I was still the newest member of the team and a foreigner. What did I know about the staff's needs?

My panic aside, the uniforms quickly had major reverberations throughout the company. And I was relieved to see they were positive. Most of the staff were unhappy about not having a uniform and had been requesting one for years now. Lately they had stopped asking because their past requests had fallen on deaf ears. I just got lucky to speak to a newer employee who didn't know any of this history.

In one fell swoop, the staff knew what we were about at Green Leaf and what they should aim toward. They were proud to come to work in their uniforms and display it to all their friends outside the company.

Customers could see the employees with their new clothes and read our motto. It gave them a sense of what we were about and helped better identify who worked in the store.

> **Lesson #3: Find ways to show the staff you're all in this together. It helps create a bond and break the differences between "management" and "line staff."**

Along with the uniforms, we ordered name badges for everyone. This reinforced the sense of pride and belonging. Perhaps because I wanted to belong, I also got myself one and wore it whenever I entered the store.

The effect was incredible. Not only was I management, but I was part of the head office which meant I was supposed to be superior to everyone else. Now here I was walking into the store with a name tag like all the other attendants. It sent a powerful message: when you're in the store, we're all equal and only there to serve customers.

That's when I knew I was starting to be accepted at Green Leaf. In the weeks ahead, I sensed a shift in how people approached me and was treated as a member of the Green Leaf family. With a uniform and a name tag, our destinies were now bound together.

RAM'S TIPS:

- To figure out what the company is about, start with where it came from. By understanding its history, you can better chart its future.

- Make sure to understand how others perceive your company. Speak to your staff, customers, suppliers, and the surrounding community. They will give you different perspectives of the value you bring them.

- Don't underestimate the power of a mission statement and a vision. The larger the company, the more important it is to spread your culture.

- Being management does not make you superior. Make sure your line staff knows that. By avoiding this perception, it will motivate everyone to focus on the main task at hand: getting more sales!

CHAPTER 7

LEARNING THE ROPES

In our first year at Harvard Business School, between the first and second term, we were put in groups for a special type of case study. Each group was a company, and the entire class made up the industry. Through our choices of which product to build, which segment to compete in, and how to price the product, our company either made a lot of money, a little, or could go bankrupt.

I can't remember exactly how it all happened, but I was the Chief Executive Officer of our little company. CEO, that sounded nice. I guess I always liked that title and must have pushed for it. Unfortunately, having the title is not sufficient for having any real leadership quality, and I sucked at it. I had great teammates but made all the wrong decisions.

The case study was meant to demonstrate the links between various departments and how they contribute to running a business. Each team member had to focus on his or her department, and the team leader, in this case, me, had to harness our strengths to propel us forward. It also showed my team how my leadership failure can lead to bankruptcy. You don't easily forget the feeling of letting everyone down.

Now here I was, six years later, thrust again into a leadership position, but I was not about to make the same mistakes. This time, instead of thrusting immediately into decision-making mode, I would take the time to listen and understand from everyone around me. Instead of pretending to "know it all," I went above and beyond to deep dive into each role and function. I wanted to know how the business worked, the current systems and processes, and what improvements, if any, we could make to realize our five-year plan and grow.

To prepare myself, in the two months between packing our things and moving from New York, I picked up all the books I could find about transitioning into a leadership role, leading family businesses, change management, and lots and lots of books about retail and grocery stores in particular. I took detailed notes from books like *The Trader Joe's Adventure*, *The 22 Immutable Laws of Marketing*, *Harvard Business Review on Change Management*, *Harvard Business Review on Strategic Marketing*, *Influence*, to name a few.

Since we had a classic tiny New York apartment and didn't have much to pack, I had lots of time to read!

Time and again, I found the most successful leaders are not made in a vacuum. They are not born with a CEO gene. Contrary to what others would have you believe, great leaders are not sitting in their office alone, contemplating the future of the industry and making big, bold bets as a result of deep self-reflection and personal analysis.

No, effective leadership starts with learning the business and listening to those keenest on seeing you succeed: your staff and your customers.

Take Sébastien Bazin from Accor, one of the largest hotel companies in the world. He took over the company in 2013 and spent the first three months visiting hotels on all five continents and having open meetings with the staff wherever he went. He did not hold a single call with investors, instead focusing his time understanding the issues and opportunities faced by his staff and managers the world over.[3]

In a way, this was similar to how I ended up learning about the Houston property market: learn first and do later. I decided the same approach would work here. I would not make a single decision the first three months of joining Green Leaf. I knew nothing about the supermarket business, so I identified each role in the company and would spend a week in the shoes of a person in that role. More importantly, I would be on the floor doing the work and not overseeing as a supervisor or simply spending time with the relevant manager of a function.

This meant I would be a cashier, a merchandiser. I would pack the goods to be sent from the warehouse to the store and receive goods sent from suppliers or the warehouse to the store. I had to do them all myself to see firsthand what it took to run this business, what challenges everyone faced, and how we could improve.

And yes, this also meant I was a bagger and learned how to properly pack lettuce.

Fun fact: I knew how to handle a till from one of my jobs while at university. So when one of the cashiers tried to teach me how to use one, they got quite the surprise when I showed them how fast I learned it! Considering how little I knew about other aspects of operating the store, the fact that I was so comfortable at the register made for a light moment.

---

3   Mozaffar Khan and George Serafeim, "Accor: Designing an Asset-Right Business and Disclosure Strategy," *HBS Case Study* no. 9-115-036 (Boston: Harvard Business School Publishing, 2015).

> **Lesson #1: No task is too small. Reading about management helps, but the real learning comes from doing every task you can find in your business.**

I learned merchandising with the help of the shelf attendants who had been doing this for fifteen years and knew intuitively what grabbed customers' attention. I spent time stocking sodas, pasta, cereals, yogurts, and having discussions to get this knowledge that they couldn't quite explain in words because they had been doing it for so long.

I learned about pricing strategies from working with Sandra to evaluate setting a sales price for new items we received. If a supplier didn't give us a recommended price, which happened for our imports, she would apply a margin on the cost based on the product category and similar items we already had on our shelves. Sometimes the look and feel of a product determined whether it should be at a premium or discounted. Part art, part science.

I learned how to fill up a truck with goods the right way from our warehouse loaders. It was important to put certain items first due to their size, which then helped maximize the number of goods that could be sent. I really had to sweat on this one!

Out of everything I did during those months, the most memorable week I spent was at the bakery.

* * *

I showed up at the store at 4:00 a.m. every morning, along with the bakery team, to help prepare bread and the morning pastries. It was hard work, and Marcus, our head baker, did not let me get off easy.

Nor did I expect him to. I wasn't a trained bread-maker and didn't expect to become one in just a week, but I did want a realistic experience working in that department. If I had joined as Marcus' trainee, what would he expect me to do?

It was important not to be treated any different, so I got the unvarnished truth on the workload and operations and demonstrated how committed I was to learning. This was not only for show. It fit directly into our five-year plan and the immediate goals Nijhad and I set for Green Leaf; how can we find areas for growth and improve the operations so we could scale better?

Officially, we would work from 4:00 a.m. until 12:00 p.m., but many days ended past 2:00 p.m. as customer orders kept coming through. Marcus and his team were so dedicated to never having an unsatisfied customer that they pushed themselves every day, taking orders for dozens of breads, varieties of pastries, and decorated birthday cakes.

What looked fun and delicious on the display was incredibly time consuming and difficult to do behind those closed doors.

First, the job was intensely physical. I spent ten-hour days standing almost the entire time, lifting twenty-kilogram bags of flour from the storage area to the bakery multiple times a day. The bags then had to be emptied into the mixer. The resulting dough had to be moved to a stainless-steel table to be rolled into shape, cut, and put into individual pans. The pans went onto a vertical rack trolley that baked dozens of breads and baguettes at the same time.

The room in which the oven was working was sweltering hot, but even though the breads were baking, you still couldn't take a break. We had to move to the pastry room and start working on cakes and sweets that could only be done in a cold room. Back and forth you'd pace all day between sweltering heat and arctic cold.

When the breads and pastries were ready, you tried not to burn your hands while taking them out of the oven and to the display area, where they cooled before being sold to customers. You couldn't use a glove for some of the more delicate breads; otherwise, they lost their shape. That wonderful smell of baked bread often comes at the expense of a few burnt fingers!

Second, each item we made required near-perfect knowledge of all the ingredients. At Green Leaf, we prized ourselves on providing variety, which meant we regularly made more than fifteen different types of bread: white, brown, sourdough, rye, olive, multi-grain, seeded, ciabatta, focaccia, brioche, and gluten-free—all in different sizes; five types of baguettes: white, brown, multi-grain, seeded, olives; a variety of pastries: plain croissant, chocolate croissant, cheese croissant, cinnamon rolls, samosas, sausage rolls; and finally, a multitude of cakes with an infinite possibility of decorations.

If I was at home, I would need to look at each recipe in a cookbook or on my phone to remember which ingredients were used for what, but Marcus knew by heart not only ingredients but the process and baking times for all of these items. He taught them to everyone on the team, including me.

"Ram, are the baguettes ready?" Marcus shouted from the other room.

"Let me check, Marcus."

He came running to me.

"What do you mean check? It's been forty-five minutes, didn't you set the timer?"

"Sorry, I thought it was sixty minutes for baguettes and forty-five minutes for the loaves."

"No, it's forty-five minutes for the baguettes, and sixty minutes for the pastries. You need to pay attention. Now this batch is ruined!"

Let's just say I felt more at ease relegated to restocking the flour bags.

Even our sales staff knew the ingredients for all the goodies we made. Customers walked in saying they were allergic to gluten, or cutting down on sugar, or couldn't have eggs because of their faith. I was so impressed to hear our employees suggesting what foods would accommodate their diet.

Third, you needed the hands of a surgeon to execute all this. A key skill for a trainee to practice was the scoring of a baguette, the process of slashing the dough with a knife to help it expand in the right direction during baking. It sounds easy, but it takes hundreds, if not thousands of attempts for any baker to perfect the technique. Sometimes my angle was off, or it was either too deep or not deep enough. I liked to think I was getting there by the end of my week though.

We also decorated cakes for birthdays and theme parties. I was in the bakery in May 2016 during the UEFA Champions League, one of the biggest European football (soccer) tournaments. We had to make cakes shaped like footballs (soccer balls), and many decorated with the Real Madrid logo and colors (one of the most popular UEFA teams in Dar). Some even needed figurines of real players on them, others had to look like a football pitch, and so on. To this day, I can't explain how Marcus and his team mixed all the right colors as they replicated even the tiniest details and made the cake look like a 3D version of what you saw on TV.

Once Marcus asked me to try to write "congratulations" on a cake. Except the cake looked too small for me to write the full word so I split it over two lines.

"Ram, what is this?"

"It's the cake you asked me to take care of, Marcus."

"Yes, I know it's the cake I gave you, but how can you write this message in two lines? Who is going to read it like this? You couldn't fit it in one line?"

"This is one of our 20cm cakes, I can't fit a fifteen-letter word on one line here."

While I was finishing my sentence, he scrapped my decoration, took the piper from my hand, and proceeded to write the word in one line and in much better cursive than I had used.

"There you go. Now, better you go get us three bags of flour. We are running out."

Marcus was a stern but patient teacher. He was not trying to make a point; he expected the same from everyone on his team, and I appreciated that.

His goal was simple, and it matched our vision—provide Green Leaf's customers the very best they could find, not only in Dar but compared to any standard. He took pride in continuously learning and improving, even sometimes from our customers who hailed from different countries and shared their preferences.

And this was the key—one of the reasons Green Leaf was so attractive to our customers. The bakery was a window into their reasons to shop in the store because of their direct interaction with the bakery staff.

Early morning customers waited outside until the store opened at 8:30 a.m. looking for fresh bread, croissants, and their morning coffee. Because production was sometimes late, we might only have yesterday's bread, but they refused, preferring to wait as long as it took to get that morning's batch.

Then those who came for a snack before lunch wanted something salty. Samosas, pies, and sausage rolls did particularly well at that time. During afternoon tea or coffee time, customers looked for a slice of cake to go along with their coffee—something sweet, but not sugary; moist, but not spongy.

One of our stores was right across from a school, and every day, at 4:00 p.m. without fail, half a dozen or so kids entered to buy a combination of candy or chips and soda. Most often, they grabbed one of every snack in the bakery display and ate it along with a smoothie or a juice while they were waiting for their parents. They were the least fussy.

Customer preferences were endless, and our strength was responding to their wishes. Our staff knew all our regular customers. They didn't know all their names, but they knew how they liked their coffee or kept aside their favorite snack if it looked like it would run out. This personal touch made a difference and helped smooth out late breads in the morning or typos on birthday cakes.

This confirmed the assessment we had made before buying the business. Green Leaf excelled at providing quality, variety, and service.

However, the behind-the-scene operations needed improvement.

Since the bakery staff had to come in early in the morning, we contracted a taxi service to help them get in on time. If the taxi was delayed, which it often was, the entire morning bread schedule was delayed.

Marcus and his team didn't receive any sales data, so each day, they guessed the previous day's sales by looking at what was left in the display and counter. If a holiday was coming up, he also had no way of knowing how many cakes were sold last year during that same holiday, which could have helped him prep for this year.

Due to space restrictions in the store, we could only keep two days' worth of flour, butter, and eggs—the main ingredients used in the bakery—in the store itself, and the rest were in the warehouse. This meant they were dependent on the store manager to place an order to the warehouse for what they needed and hoped it would come on time. It often wouldn't, and production had to stop for an hour while someone called the warehouse and made an urgent appeal for the missing ingredient.

All of these holes in our operation were made clearer during my time working in the bakery department. If I could help ensure the taxi service was there on time every day, provide them direct access to the sales figures, and give them autonomy to order from the warehouse, their administrative load would lessen and they could focus even more on providing the best to our customers.

These changes didn't cost money, but they did require more thoughtfulness. And it could lead directly to both increased profits and employee satisfaction, as we could reduce wastage, lost sales, and coordination headaches for staff.

* * *

I showed up every day and did what I was told. It was awkward for some of the staff, as I was supposed to be their boss, but here they were showing me how to best display sodas based on the type of bottle and size, or how to print and put price stickers on the shelves. I did all the work and observed diligently.

I also got to know the staff better along with their hopes and aspirations. Rehema, the same cashier who tried to teach me how to use a till, had recently graduated from night school, earning an accounting degree. She was looking for another job where she could earn more and use what she had studied. Since she was hard-working, meticulous, and well respected in her position, I thought, *"We have to find a way to keep her!"* Balendra was actually looking for a new team member in Accounts, but because there was no internal communication, Rehema had no idea.

I told her about the opening, and she applied and got the job. Not only did we retain a strong employee, but this also had a huge impact on my ability to build relationships with staff and for them to feel comfortable sharing their life goals with me.

This led to the most important realization I ever had during my time at Green Leaf: by participating in all these tasks, by listening, by sweating this small stuff, I realized not only what changes needed to be made to improve our operations but also that all changes were possible as long as I had the staff's trust.

> **Lesson #2: Earning trust is as important as understanding the business.**

By working alongside and enduring the same joys and hardships that went with the workday, I got to know them as people and not just numbers on a spreadsheet. This helped me gain their trust, and that trust led me to become an effective leader in the organization.

As much as I enjoyed having the title of CEO, it was nothing compared to having the respect of the team. It was now my team, and I was ready to lead them.

RAM'S TIPS:

- Sweat the small stuff! Go all in to really understand how operations work at all levels of the company.

- Don't make assumptions upfront about what you think works or doesn't, what you can or should improve. Let yourself be guided by the work and the process. After all, if things are done a certain way, there must be a reason. Figure out the reason and then decide what to do.

- Earning trust is not easy, but it's the key to being a successful leader.

CHAPTER 8

TIME FOR A BREAK

Nearly six months had elapsed since we first touched ground at Julius Nyerere International Airport in what would be our new lives.

I was starting to feel overwhelmed by everything I saw, by how much I had learned, but also by how much still needed to be understood. I only had work on my mind, which, incidentally, is why Neha decided to book our first vacation.

> **Lesson #1: You are still only human. Remember to take a break before you burn out.**

Tanzania is not very well-known. World news about Africa generally focuses on stories of violence or military coups, so it's no wonder that the country doesn't come up much in conversations. It certainly never came up in *Progressive Grocer*, one of the leading newsletters about all things supermarket, to which I had just gotten a subscription.

Tanzania is a peaceful country, and its economy—ranked 78th in the world by the IMF—is driven by agriculture and gold mining.[4]

Even if you haven't heard much about it, you're likely to have heard of its legendary trio of natural wonders without possibly realizing where they were. First, the Serengeti, home to the Great Migration, which sees over three million antelopes cross crocodile-infested rivers to reach the lush plains of Northern Tanzania. Second, the snowcapped Mount Kilimanjaro, the highest mountain in Africa and the highest single free-standing mountain in the world. And finally, Zanzibar, with its turquoise blue waters, spice fragrance, and a name that just invokes relaxation.

We decided to go on a safari to the Serengeti and spend seven days away from Dar, which, if you listened to our tour guide, was still not enough to see everything. We were skeptical, wrongly, but since we lived in Dar, we figured we could come back whenever we wanted.

The trip was unbelievable.

First, we went to Lake Manyara, where we spent the day watching a flamboyance of flamingos—that's the actual term for a group of the birds. We also got lucky and saw a group of tree-climbing lions.

Then we descended into Ngorongoro. Three million years ago, a gigantic volcano exploded with such force it collapsed onto itself, in the process creating the largest intact caldera in the world. It covers an area of 260 square kilometers, equivalent to forty football fields, and the rim of the crater sits at an altitude of 2,400 meters. When you start making your way

---

4   "World Economic Outlook Database, October 2019," International Monetary Fund, accessed September 19, 2020.

down to the bottom of the caldera, a drop of more than 600 meters, you are rewarded with the most breathtaking views of this ecosystem. If you're lucky, you can see the endangered black rhino or meet a pack of lions and all sorts of wildlife that rarely leaves the safety and lushness of the crater.

Finally, we arrived at the Serengeti, meaning the "endless plains" in the local Maasai language. Spanning thirty thousand square kilometers, it truly felt endless. We saw elephants, lions, leopards, cheetahs, buffaloes, zebras, and countless other animals. During our three days there, we encountered them repeatedly, but every time felt like it was our first. Even when they were just lying in the sun napping, it was mesmerizing to watch. And the moment they got up, we got excited—every single time!

I am glad no one watches me the same way while I'm napping!

* * *

This vacation was a time to relax and a time to learn. While a safari experience isn't a window into Tanzanian culture, we found that conversations went a long way. Whether it was learning about the magnificence of the baobab tree while enjoying sundowners with a *konyagi* (a local gin) and tonic, learning about the health benefits of *moringa* (a regional tree with lots of vitamins and minerals), or watching the sunrise with a hot cup of Tanzanian coffee and *mandazi* (fried dough magic), we covered politics to history, language to geography, and made new friends along the way.

At this time, we were also taking weekly Swahili classes and were keen on trying it out during our trip.

Our guide and driver greeted us every morning, *Karibu wageni!* ("Welcome visitors!"). *Karibu* is the warmest welcome word you can find. It is said with a large smile, displaying as many teeth as possible. You say it to welcome a guest at home, a colleague into your office, or customers entering the store. It also means "you're welcome" and "come again"! So you also use it as customers pay for their goods and thank the bagger, and then again when they leave the store to make sure they come back.

Habari za asubuhi? I replied, asking him how he was doing, or, more literally, "How is the news of the morning?" You always reply *Habari* once somebody welcomes you. You can use it by itself or with a modifier like *Habari za leo?* (How is your day?) or *Habari za mchana?* (How is your afternoon?). Neha and I later learned to use the more informal *mambo vipi* with people we knew well.

Safi. Na wewe?

Fine. And you?

Mimi pia, asante.

Me too, thanks.

Safi, asante. Swahili is full of words short in letters but big in conveying emotions. Another word we used often was *pole,* which means "sorry." Pole can be used if you're on the street and people are in your way, if you accidentally bump someone and want to apologize, and all the way to expressing your deepest condolences.

Every morning brought new excitement when we met our safari driver.

"*Karibu wageni,* what would you like to see today?"

That was a running joke among all the game park drivers. We were in the wild and animals did not appear on demand.

"We've seen so many lions yesterday; let's do something else today," I replied.

Neha invariably added, "Giraffes, let's find more giraffes!"

"*Pole*, the giraffes are on vacation today, but we can see elephants instead."

You'd think lions were the hardest to find, but try spotting a giraffe when all the grass around is the same color!

* * *

In my four years living in Tanzania, I can tell you one thing: if we judged a country not by the size of its GDP but by the warmth of its people, Tanzania would, hands down, be among the G7 group of major developed countries.

People appreciate your presence. When you are in a restaurant or hotel, you are made to feel like you always belonged, like you were expected the whole time and now that you are here, everything can start. It's an amazing feeling, and you need to be there to experience it.

Disconnecting for a few days was a great idea, and our first vacation in the country was extraordinary. When doing business in a new country or across borders, you often forget that the soft aspects are as important as the facts and figures.

Seeing the beauty of the country, meeting more people, this was all a chance to understand better the history and the geography that made it what it was. And if you understand the context, you can better see its future.

I felt relaxed and started to realize I needed to balance my life and work better to truly enjoy what I was doing. There was still a lot of work, but now I was also looking forward to all the other trips we could take. Our move wasn't only about improving margins but also about growing personally. Travel can teach you a lot, especially when you're willing and open to learning.

I was glad to have had this time off. It cleared my head and helped me better understand the key items I needed to focus on in our next phase. In the previous six months, I had seen what worked but also what we could improve. It was time to start making those improvements.

RAM'S TIPS:

- Don't forget about work-life balance, ideally before burn-out sets in! It's important to take time away from the business; incidentally, it will also provide perspective on what really matters (business-wise and personally).

PART 2

MANAGE
& GROW

"Think big, act small."

CHAPTER 9

THE MEETING

———

Between business school and Green Leaf, there was another time I was in charge, when I worked with a development team in Surat, India to get a shopping center built. During the final three months of construction, I was there to help lead it to opening day by accelerating decision-making between headquarters in Mumbai and the staff on the ground.

We had the construction, leasing, marketing, finance, HR, and IT teams on-site all getting prepped for the big day, but we still had a lot to do. Because I came at the end of the project, everyone already had a level of understanding between them. They all worked well together and, being in one office, could communicate effectively and quickly among themselves.

Here are a few issues we had to deal with:

- We used a top-up card system for all the restaurants in the food court, but the smaller mom-and-pop shops did not know how the system worked and did not trust the funds to be transferred in time. How could we convince them it was in everyone's interest to follow the same protocol?

- A clothing store thought it was situated too close to one of its competitors. Could we reshuffle other tenants to give them a different space?

- We had three anchor tenants, and they were fighting to have their logo appear the biggest on the outside wall. What could be considered fair?

- How could we go about training the hundreds of staff we needed to run the center?

All these were finishing problems, and although not always easy to fix, I was surrounded by a motivated and cohesive team ready to tackle the problem from every angle to find the best solution together.

* * *

As I reflected on all the issues I saw these past few months in Dar, my experience in Surat was coming back to me. How did we manage to get such a huge and complex project done on time? There were so many decisions with so many options. What did we do right?

The common thread between all the issues I heard at Green Leaf was communication. People worked in silos and did what was best for themselves.

This meant that the best ideas in one store were never seen by other stores. You could have a great Easter display put together by Neema in the Peninsula branch, but over at the Bongoyo Road branch, no one would have heard about it.

Or the warehouse would suddenly find that a case of mayonnaise expired this month. They sent it straight to the closest store in Kimweri, which already had an excess, without realizing the Peninsula branch had run out completely.

These issues happened all the time. Instead of using our scale to our advantage, each store was running as an independent fiefdom and didn't care to know what others were doing.

I spent nearly three-quarters of my time in the stores and started to get a good sense of what sold better in each. I also started noticing when a product was in big quantity in one store but was certain to run out shortly in another. When I saw such things, I took pictures and messaged them to the other store managers to ask if they needed it. Most of the time the answer was yes, as I had guessed, and we arranged for one of our vans to coordinate the transfer.

When I saw a nice display at Bongoyo, I took a picture and went to the Kimweri branch to show our staff what the other branch had done. They loved getting those ideas and would do the same or try to do even better.

This gave me an idea. Instead of me serving as an intermediary, why not create a WhatsApp group with all the stores so everyone could see what everyone else was doing?

Initially, we had only one for the branch managers and myself, but I quickly realized it was not enough. That group was good to send stock around the branches, but not much else, so we created another one between the warehouse and receiving managers to push and pull stock around. Then we did another one with the head merchandisers of each store so they could exchange photos of their product display. Finally, we had another one between our bakers in different stores so they could share recipes and cake decoration tips.

> **Lesson #1: By using WhatsApp, we were able to accelerate spreading best practices in the company.**

* * *

In the beginning, I was doing all the picture taking and sharing. No one wanted to put their names out there, thinking what they shared was not important and that others would make fun of them for being unable to sell certain products.

A long weekend was coming up with a public holiday that Friday. Nane Nane, which means "eight eight," is celebrated on August 8 every year. It recognizes the important contribution of farmers to the Tanzanian economy, so we usually made displays of gift baskets with a theme around agriculture and farming.

That Thursday, I showed up at the Peninsula store but left my phone in the car on purpose. Neha had been to the store that morning and told me of the nice display they had done. I was keen on replicating the same in the other stores, so when I walked in, I immediately told Neema, the assistant manager in charge of displays, that I wanted to share it on our WhatsApp group.

"Oh, oh, I can't find my phone."

"Oh no, sir, was it stolen? Did it happen in the store? Quick, let us call security."

"No no, Neema, don't worry. I remember I left it in the office. It's ok, but we need to share this with the other branches. Do you have your phone with you?"

"Ugh no, sir, I don't come to the floor with it."

She must have sensed what was coming because she started to take a few steps away from me. I wouldn't let her go so easily.

"Ok, can you bring it please? Why don't you take a photo and send it to me so I can share it with the group?"

My lie worked and she was relieved. She went to the office, grabbed her phone, and came back to take a few pictures. She showed them to me.

"Is this ok to send you, sir?"

"Yes, it's good, but since you're sending them to me, just send them directly on the group to avoid the extra step."

She was cornered. She had her phone out and the pictures taken and ready to be sent. There was no excuse now; she couldn't back off and had to send them to the group. She was anxious, sweating in anticipation of the responses (or lack thereof) she would get from sharing them. That feeling didn't last long.

"Neema, this display is amazing. Congratulations!" read the first message.

Another one came within seconds: "Oh wow, super display, Neema! I told my guys, and they are doing the same right now."

The shyness turned into pride. My little trick worked and started a chain reaction of everyone in the WhatsApp group communicating directly with each other. After all, it made more sense to have the branches talk to each other. They knew what sold and what didn't better than anyone else, so having them take this responsibility of exchanging ideas and products was for the best.

Of course, I was a bit concerned that people replied so quickly on their phones, but one problem at a time.

The creation of group messaging helped spread positive ideas faster between the teams, but that was not the only communication problem we had.

* * *

People still worked in silos and sometimes made decisions without informing anyone else. Unfortunately, what made someone's life easy did not necessarily translate to everyone else, and often it was just the opposite.

For example, the Procurement team would get a promotion from our supplier. If we bought double our normal quantities, we would get a big discount. They processed the order without ever informing the Accounts team. When Accounts received the invoice, they were furious because they had not budgeted for it and now didn't have the funds planned for such a big order. It might have made sense from a commercial point of view, but perhaps not when you take into account our bank costs.

The supplier, in turn, sent angry emails to Accounts asking for the payments they were promised, and our following orders would not be honored. What should have been a win-win became a nightmare situation to manage.

At lunch with Neha, after getting wind of such an incident for the third time that month, I told her about it.

"So you're saying that Kabir from Procurement decides on his own to buy more quantities of a product without checking in with anyone?" Neha repeated.

"Yes, that's right."

"And he doesn't even check with you? Don't you get a notice of the order at least?"

"Hmm, no I don't... why should I?"

"Well, you're the CEO of the business. You should empower people to make decisions in the normal course of business, and of course, if they're in alignment with the company's mission statement, but I don't think this action from Kabir falls under either, so why aren't you consulted?"

"I guess I'm not in the Procurement decision-making."

After a short pause, I added "You're right. Perhaps I should integrate myself into the procurement process and check every order that is outside of the normal course of business."

"Well, for starters, duh! But also, that's only giving you more work. In any case, you can't make that decision by yourself. You need Balendra's help from Accounts."

"Yes, but there's a weird tension between everyone, and I'm not sure how I can get those two to communicate."

"Why don't you guys discuss it at your next executive meeting?"

I must have looked at Neha like a deer in the headlights when she said those last two words. In all these months, we never had a meeting with all the senior leadership. How was that possible?

I had been so busy running from store to store that talking individually with each manager felt like I'd had a meeting with everyone... which, of course, was not the case!

Neha added, "If you haven't had a meeting all this time, it says a lot about the leadership vacuum in the company and explains why people work in silos."

That was so true. The various departments lacked cohesive decision-making, and we held no strategy meeting to decide on the direction of the company or talk about short-term and long-term goals and, most importantly, where we resolved our differences.

* * *

We had to organize this meeting, and do it fast. That Thursday afternoon, I called Balendra (Finance & Accounts), Kabir (Procurement), Kondo (IT), Samir (Warehouse), Marcus

(Bakery), Sandra (Pricing), and Ali and Jeremy (Store Managers) and told them to come to the office the following Thursday afternoon for a meeting.

Although this meeting was long overdue, I still needed a few days to organize a game plan. It was critical that the meeting go in the right direction; otherwise, I could end up making things much worse.

I needed to establish centralized leadership without anyone feeling like their powers were taken away. At the same time, I wanted to empower people to figure out how to solve problems among themselves, which required them to get on the same page and communicate. Considering how much infighting had been built up over the years, was that even possible? Could they move away from years of passive-aggressive behavior?

I leafed through my Leadership class notes from business school. We had learned about five different types of power a manager can exhibit:[5]

- Positional – derived from your authority

- Coercive – ability to punish

- Reward – ability to confer value

- Expert – through your skills, expertise, and experience

- Referent – through your personality & charisma

---

5   Heidi K. Gardner, "Leadership and Organizational Behavior" (lecture, Harvard Business School, Boston, MA, Fall 2009).

Being the CEO, I automatically had the first three. My title gave me authority, and I could punish or reward employees by firing them or giving them bigger bonuses at the end of the year. I didn't have too much expert power yet, except perhaps in the field of finance. And I had never heard anyone call me charismatic before, so scratch that! But as I read that definition more, I realized it was as linked to personality as to the trust derived from it.

I didn't have a full jar of the last two, but I was building my experience and had gained a lot of trust by working all those jobs in each store.

I think I have all five. Now what to do with that power? Having it is not an end in and of itself. You need to use it in times of crisis or instability, to fill a void in authority, when you see things out of balance with your values, or if there are conflicts. You use it to influence people to get the outcomes you need. In this case, it means that from the power you wield, people listen and trust what you tell them. You can push them to work toward a common goal, yours. That's the panacea of effective leadership, and I needed some tools to give me more confidence and eventually drive the changes we needed.

In class, we had gone through a dozen or so principles that help us gain influence, but those that marked me the most were:[6]

- Build trusting relationships: one of the best strategies is to use active listening. It helps you gain power via information acquisition and trust and does not give away power (contrary to what people think when they ask questions related to topics they don't know about).

---

6   Amy Cuddy, "Power and Influence" (lecture, Harvard Business School, Boston, MA, Fall 2010).

- Be the change: walk the walk of who you want to be.

- Be a lovable star: project both warmth and competence. Being the smartest person in the room isn't enough or even necessary if you're not trusted.

Ok, so if I had those three things, along with the power identified above, I could influence the outcome. Next, I needed one more tool from my class to resolve disputes. The key to managing conflicts is the concept of advocacy vs. inquiry.[7] Managers are trained to be advocates for themselves as they are rewarded for decision-making. They are not usually rewarded for inquiry or asking questions about how things can work or improve.

We needed to achieve in this meeting a balance of advocacy—ensuring all voices are heard about the issues faced in each department—and inquiry—asking colleagues how a team's decision impacts their department's work. How is it done? By using the Ladder of Inference. Put simply, it means we all look at the same data, select the metric that matters, interpret it, and draw a conclusion from it.[8]

Dramatically different conclusions can be reached from the same data, but that's the point. We all approach problems from a different angle, and it has nothing to do with personality but, rather, where we sit in the organization and the situation we are facing.

Now it was time for the show.

---

7   Heidi K. Gardner, "Leadership and Organizational Behavior" (lecture, Harvard Business School, Boston, MA, Fall 2009).

8   Ibid.

* * *

Before the meeting, I told everyone who the participants were and that we would focus on ways to reduce stock-outs. They should come ready with ideas and ready to vigorously debate them. I was somewhat vague so no one would feel like they were targeted but also gave enough direction so everyone had something to prepare.

I also didn't want to give specific sales goals or cost reductions. I remembered an article I read about when Paul O'Neill became the CEO of Alcoa, the aluminum manufacturing giant, in October 1987. Investors were nervous since Alcoa had faltered with failed product lines, but when O'Neill met with them, he didn't talk about profit margins or revenue projections. Instead, he talked about worker safety. "Every year, numerous Alcoa workers are injured so badly that they miss a day of work," O'Neill stated. "I intend to make Alcoa the safest company in America. I intend to go for zero injuries."[9]

Investors in the room immediately fled to their telephones to sell their stock and advise everyone they knew to do the same, but they didn't understand that fundamentally rethinking the approach to safety led to managers rethinking dozens of systems and processes they had in place. And forcing that rethink led to an increase in the bottom line.[10]

Over O'Neill's tenure, Alcoa dropped from 1.86 lost workdays to injury per 100 workers to 0.2. One year after O'Neill's speech, the company's profits hit a record high. When he

---

9   Drake Baer, "How Changing One Habit Helped Quintuple Alcoa's Income," *Business Insider,* April 9, 2014.

10 Ibid.

retired thirteen years later, Alcoa's annual net income was five times higher than when he started.[11]

That's what I was going for with reducing stock-outs.

As that Thursday afternoon approached, I was getting nervous. It was not an exaggeration to say the fate of the entire company and our vision for the next five years depended on this meeting going well.

* * *

It didn't start well at all.

There were nine of us, but our only meeting space was an area right outside my office with a small glass round table that could seat, at most, five people. As people walked in, there was already a power play as to who would be sitting at the table right next to me and who would be left standing.

The air conditioning was going at full blast, but in the hot Dar es Salaam weather, even in the cooler month of August, you could see beads of sweat rolling down everyone's face. It might have been the heat or the anxiety of being called into this meeting next to the CEO's office, who just spent the last six months trying to figure out all the things going wrong in the company.

I couldn't start on such a bad note and definitely didn't want anyone to feel like those sitting at the table had a more important voice than others. So I got up and ran out.

No, I didn't run away from the meeting! I simply went over to the store and got a cold soda for everyone. Then got one of the staff to help me bring additional chairs from the Accounts office.

---

11 Ibid.

Now we had eight chairs, so instead of one of the managers standing, I decided it would be me.

If I didn't have any referent power before, this would surely help!

Now we were all settled, and there was a deafening silence. The atmosphere was so tense you could cut a knife through it. I could see Kabir looking down at his feet, almost waiting to be singled out. Ali looked annoyed to be there. He was the only one to ask me how long the meeting would be, as he had lots of things to do at the store.

Sandra looked perplexed as to why she was included in this meeting. She had an important role, some would say the most important, as it determined the profit we made on each product. But somehow, she never felt like she was part of leadership. Then again, since there never were any such meetings before, no one was part of leadership.

The only relaxed person in the room was Kondo from IT. He was always jovial, and everyone in the company trusted him. I'd had a good chat with him the previous day about this meeting.

Although most people in the room had started to trust me, they clearly did not always trust each other.

To break the ice, I started by doing a round of introductions and asking everyone to tell one story they heard or saw of a positive customer experience and a negative one. The introductions were silly since everyone knew each other, but I thought it would be an easy way to ensure everyone spoke at least once.

We went around the room, starting with Jeremy, then Kondo, Balendra, Sandra, and then Ali. He had a good positive story, but the negative one started the personal attacks.

"I had a customer who came in yesterday and requested sparkling water. I have been asking Kabir to order and send me more, but every time he sends me small quantities, and so many customers leave disappointed."

Kabir didn't wait for his turn to reply.

"Ali, you place orders directly with the supplier without informing me. I told you many times the supplier doesn't have that many in stock and we have to split this between all the stores."

"And I told you, Kabir, my store is the best performing one so you should send me all the stock. I can sell them, but right now so many of my customers leave disappointed. Next time, I will just pay the supplier cash out of that day's sales and I will show you we can sell more."

Hearing this clear contravention of cash policy, Balendra leaped up from his seat.

"You can't do that. Don't use cash to pay for suppliers; that is difficult to track and can lead to a double payment."

Kabir muttered under his breath, "Typical," except in such a small space, it easily echoed through the entire room and Balendra started turning red.

"What do you mean typical? All of you think our job in Accounts is only to stop you, but we have to report the sales and profit of the business. We have to justify all your purchases and deal with all the suppliers. None of you ever tell us, 'There was such and such issue, so the cash balance did not reconcile for that day.' Instead, we have to look at the files you send us three days late and reconcile everything manually. Think about our difficulties."

Things were spiraling out of control. I had to say something and see if we could practice some inquiry.

"Yes, actually you all bring up a good point. We are clearly missing sales, as Ali said, but if the supplier doesn't have the product, then what? There is a process for a reason, so we can't just circumvent it. What else can be done?"

Silence again. Kabir, Balendra, and Ali's face were red with anger. To defuse the tension, I volunteered Sandra into the conversation as a neutral third party.

"Sandra, what do you think?"

"Me, Mr. Ram?"

"Yes, you Sandra. You know all the products we have in the system. Is there something else we could do for our customers?"

"Actually, Mr. Ram, we used to import this sparkling water. It sold very well, and the profit margin was higher, but I'm not sure why we stopped importing it."

"Kabir, you know all about our imports. Do you know why we don't bring it anymore?"

"Actually, we still do, but we have this customer, a high-end lodge in the Serengeti. Whatever stock we have, they buy it all. So we're never left with anything for the stores."

"Balendra, is that right?"

"Yes, that is right. Once I even spoke to their Accounts guy and he said that they would even be willing to pay a deposit if we brought in more."

"Balendra, did you share this information with Kabir? Kabir, did you know that?"

Before Kabir could say anything, Balendra replied, "No, I didn't. I should have and I'm sorry."

There it was. A turning point. The realization that a mistake was made.

Balendra continued, "Actually, after I spoke to that person, we had these auditors from the Labor Department to check our employee records. I was so tired at the end of the day, so it completely skipped my mind to inform Kabir."

And now they realized the mistake was not personal. Balendra had a lot on his plate. On top of doing all the accounts work, he dealt with various ministries who often come to do spot checks—whether the tax authority, immigration department, occupational health and safety, food and drug board, or, in this case, the labor department—he dealt with them all in the background so everyone else could do their work in peace.

Kabir quickly picked up from there.

"It's ok. It happens. You do a lot, and I also sometimes fail to tell you when I speak to suppliers and negotiate with them. From now on, if it's ok, I will come by your office once a week so we can update each other."

They themselves figured out that communication was the key. The breakdown of communication had led to mistrust and suspicion among them, and they were keen to resolve it. We had a breakthrough.

Ali was still not convinced since we hadn't formally resolved his problem of missing sparkling water, but that's when I thought my conversation with Kondo the previous day would pay off.

I had anticipated the meeting would be tense and wanted to find a win, something everyone could easily rally around and that would break the cycle of mistrust. Kondo had been trying to make everyone's life easier with some of his solutions for our IT system, but it never went anywhere because there was no leadership to back him up either with capital or pushing it to the teams.

I gave him the floor, and he put an Excel report he had created on the screen.

"I wanted to show everyone a dashboard of our sales figures per store for the last month. You can see the sales per store and per category. This can immediately give you a sense of what is selling and how fast."

Jeremy raised his hand with a question.

"We have seen this before; it is not helpful because the categories are all wrong and the sales data is never up to date."

Kondo had anticipated the argument.

"With Mr. Ram's help, we spent the last few months cleaning up the entire database. Now you will see all products are properly categorized and we even reordered all the categories so they make more sense. Also, we have been working on an automated module, so as soon as you turn off the system at night with the day's sales closed, it automatically uploads the information to this dashboard so you can see all this by the next morning when you arrive at the store."

The looks on everyone's face was priceless. They didn't know such a thing was possible. Kondo had been lobbying Amir to do this for many years, but without success. Amir was old school and operated with his gut, preferring to visit each store to figure out what was selling and what was not. That worked when there was one store to manage, but with the scale of operations now and the technology available, you needed to complement physical visits with actual data.

While we were recategorizing the database, Kondo came up with this solution and I gave him the budget to execute it. Now here we were with an effective solution everyone could use.

Balendra could check the sales amount from the prior day and compare it to the cash deposited in the bank accounts. With updated real-time sales information, Kabir could see what products were selling and place orders. Ali and Jeremy could deep dive by category for their stores to check what was moving. And with the weekly sales information, Sandra could verify that the price she assigned for certain products was not too high or too low whenever she had any doubts.

This was a win for all, and the idea had been sitting there this whole time. While we talked about the benefits of this report for everyone, it also helped the managers hear and learn about the other functions within the company—what they did, why this helped them, and what else they could do with this new information. Communication was finally happening. This meeting was a real turning point, and despite the difficult start, it ended up going even better than I expected.

All these seemed simple in retrospect, but years of communication neglect resulted in people developing their own internal procedures disregarding the organization's overall needs. Without communication, everyone thinks the other person is out to "get them," as absurd as that sounds.

The executive meeting helped start a change in mindset. Getting this new report was important, but even more critical was the simple fact of establishing healthy and effective communication. Having others with whom you could share your issues, and knowing they have your back, helped you feel more connected to your work, which meant better decision-making.

That's what effective leadership combined with open communication was all about. Managers were less stressed, the different departments were interacting, morale was on the rise, and people were smiling again. Well, this is Tanzania, they never stopped smiling, but at least they had one more reason to do so.

RAM'S TIPS:

- Finding ways to accelerate communication will encourage the spread of best practices across the company.

- A manager can exhibit five types of power: positional, coercive, reward, expert, and referent. Figure out which ones you have and which you need to work on.

- To gain influence as a leader, build trusting relationships within the company, be the change you want to implement, be a lovable star, and project warmth and competence.

- Don't play the blame game. Use the concept of advocacy and inquiry, and the Ladder of Inference, to find ways to move forward.

- Use all of the above in your leadership meetings to pursue your goals!

CHAPTER 10

FAILURE AND SUCCESS

—

After the successful conclusion of our first executive meeting, I felt like I was hitting a stride. I was looking at other changes we could make in the business, listening to ideas from everyone, and seeing what could be implemented.

I hadn't done much yet, but it was all in planning. There was no deadline or strong impetus for change, except my own self-motivation for giving it all I had and becoming the best supermarket chain we could be.

That is my personality; give it my all and show what I'm capable of. I always want to be the best. Well... actually, not always.

* * *

During my sophomore year of high school, I realized I could do more. I could do better if not be the best in class—not just the best in a vanity project to tower over everyone else, but the best in terms of what I could do, how much I could push myself, and not being satisfied until I felt like I gave it my all.

I grew up in Guadeloupe, a beautiful island in the Caribbean and a part of France. Toward the end of that school year and depending on their grades, students could choose what subjects they wanted to specialize in—math, social sciences, or literature.

- Math was known to be the most academically challenging.

- Social Sciences was a little less challenging academically and what most students would choose.

- Literature was for those gifted with the written word.

Now, I know you're reading a book I wrote, but trust me when I tell you this. At that time, I could not write to save my life! I chose math.

As I said, it's not enough to want it; you also need the grades for it. So once done with all our exams for the year, Mrs. Pierrette, my grade teacher, pulled me aside and said I could qualify for the math specialization, but barely.

I had good overall grades, which helped, but she worried I'd be unable to cope with the harder topics and workload that came with the next two years of studies.

She gave me a choice. I could go on with the math program and hope for the best, although I would likely struggle, or pick the social sciences specialization, where I would be more likely to do well given my grades.

I felt like such a letdown. I thought I was good in school, never the top student but consistently in the top quartile, which I believed set me up well. This was not the case, and this conversation with Mrs. Pierrette opened my eyes.

But I knew something else; I had not been giving it my all and could do better. I had to do better but not to prove her wrong. On the contrary, she was right! If I continued this way, I would struggle and likely fail. I knew I had to put in more effort and I had it in me somewhere, but it just never occurred to me that I had to try harder, work harder, and study longer hours to get better grades.

In truth, I was afraid. I was afraid I wasn't good enough and would fail. It was easier not to try too hard to avoid feeling emotionally connected to the results.

And so I chose to not be afraid anymore and try harder. I chose the math specialization for my junior and senior year. I worked every day during recess, lunchtime, on the bus coming and going from school, as soon as I got home, and until late at night. I realized that, fundamentally, there were no hard problems, just solutions that required more creative thinking. And when I was stuck on a problem at night, my mind kept thinking about it while I was sleeping. By the time I woke up the next day, I could often visualize a path to the solution.

The next year, Mrs. Pierrette was so impressed by my increased performance that she asked what happened to me.

I told her the truth. "You were right to say I would struggle, but you made me realize I had more in me to give, and that's what I did."

So when Ali, the branch manager of our biggest and most profitable branch, sent me a text message late on a Friday night saying he was quitting, I felt again that same sense of urgency.

* * *

Up until then, I had been working hard at learning the business, holding meetings individually and with the various teams, and being a sponge for all the information I was getting a hold of. The machine was running smoothly, and there was no reason to rock the boat too much. A few improvements here and there, like recategorization of data and some updates to the reports, and all was going well.

One day in September, I was walking through our Peninsula branch and talking to the staff in anticipation of the weekend. It was back-to-school season, which not only meant students were buying new books and stationery for the year but also that families coming back from vacation stocked up on all food essentials.

One of our biggest sales weeks of the year after Christmas was starting this weekend. We needed to be ready with all our goods and displays by Thursday for the mass of shoppers coming in.

As I was walking around the store, one of the staff came up and waved me aside. He wanted to share something but didn't want anyone else to hear what he was about to say. We went over near the freezer area where the sound from the machines usually helped cover conversations.

"Sir, you have to check the cameras for yesterday."

"Why?"

"Because, sir, just check the cameras, especially at the back of the store, and you will see."

I knew the staff didn't like to tell on their colleagues, but I also didn't like being sent on a wild goose chase not knowing what I was supposed to look for, if there was even anything.

> **Lesson #1: Don't engage in gossip. If someone comes to you for information, tell them you will keep everything confidential, but they need to be clear about what they are telling you and that you will need a way to verify it.**

"Please tell me what it is. I don't know what to look for and it will take me hours to go through everything. Just tell me and I won't share with anyone; I promise."

Shifting his eyes left to right to make sure no one was watching us, he told me discreetly that an incident had happened in the store the previous day—something no one dared to share.

Sandeep, the manager responsible for receiving and checking products, had come to work drunk.

He was so belligerently drunk that he started cursing the staff. This was before the store opened for trading, so there were no customer witnesses, but everyone else on the morning shift saw it happen and felt threatened. Sandeep is not particularly big, but he was being verbally abusive, and a few times, he even held a stick and swung it around in a threatening manner.

The other managers in the store tried to calm him down, but he was too erratic to be reasoned with. Finally, Ali, the branch manager, arrived, and also tried to calm Sandeep. It didn't go well, and although no one knew exactly what happened, you could hear Sandeep crying. Ali put him in a taxi and sent him home.

That was shocking to hear. I never imagined such behavior from Sandeep, and I was glad Ali managed to send him home, but even more shocking was that this was not the first time.

Since I joined, it sounded like this had happened half a dozen times at least, and every time, Ali had managed to take control of the situation. But why wasn't Ali saying anything to me or anyone in management? Surely you wouldn't want one of your key staff members to regularly show up drunk to work and threaten everyone?

I was puzzled by all this. This was not acceptable behavior from Sandeep, but why was Ali covering it up?

I decided to confide in Balendra and get some advice on how to handle this. That's when he gave me more alarming news.

Sandeep and Ali were related, and that's likely why he kept covering it up. Ali didn't want Sandeep to lose his job, so he made sure to not tell anyone about these incidents. And because they were family, he wanted to keep Sandeep near him, despite our policy at Green Leaf that family members should work in different stores.

Balendra only found out by chance, scrolling through Facebook and seeing a photo of the two of them with a caption that made it clear they were brothers-in-law. He hadn't told anyone, not knowing how to approach the situation and not wanting to get his friend Ali in trouble for hiding this information.

Something had to be done.

Hiding the family links was problematic. We had people come through references all the time, and often they were family relatives. Our policy in these cases was simple. It is mandatory to disclose the relationship, and we assign each staff to different stores to avoid any potential intrigue.

In addition, both Sandeep's behavior and Ali's handling of the situation were seriously concerning.

I had lunch with Neha that day and told her what happened that morning.

"So, what are you going to do?" she asked.

"Well, if I knew, I would have told you already!" I snapped. I was a bit too stressed about this and the outcomes I was seeing in front of me did not look good.

"Ok, well for starters, have you spoken to Ali about this?"

"No, I haven't. I'm not sure how he will react and what he will say."

"You can't control what he will say or do or deny, but you have the facts and you need to talk to him."

"Yes, but we're on the verge of the back-to-school season. That branch makes 40 percent of our sales, and Ali is our best performing manager. What if his work suffers?"

"Ram, this goes beyond that. Maybe the sales will suffer this weekend because Ali is not focused. Or maybe this ruins your working relationship forever, but can you live with yourself knowing that the staff is placed in a position where they feel threatened? Is that really the right thing to do?"

She was absolutely right. I was hesitant because I was still afraid I had so much to learn about the business. I still didn't feel right making big decisions, and disciplining Ali would have strong repercussions. It had to be done, though, and I couldn't shy away from it.

Neha added, "Look, the reality is Ali made a mistake, but he was trying to protect his family. Maybe he keeps hoping that Sandeep will change, but he hasn't."

"Let's see how it plays out. Wish me luck."

* * *

That was on a Thursday, Ali's day off. I could have called Ali into my office, but that felt patronizing and intimidating. When dealing with difficult personal situations, it is important to put the other person at ease, preferably in an environment they are comfortable in. The next morning, I walked into the store and asked to speak to Ali in his office. I got straight to the point.

> **Lesson #2:** If you're about to have a difficult conversation with someone, try to have it on their turf or in a neutral zone so they don't feel cornered. Nobody likes to be called to the principal's office.

"Ali, I heard there was an incident with Sandeep a few days ago. What happened?"

Ali looked at me perplexed, seemingly not knowing what I was talking about. "No sir, nothing happened."

I had to be careful to protect my source. He had come to me in confidence, knowing full well he would face retribution for divulging such sensitive information.

"I happened to be looking at the store cameras two days ago, and I saw Sandeep acting violently toward the staff. He was shouting at them for almost an hour until you finally arrived and sent him home."

"Oh, that, sir! No, it was nothing. He was just in a bad mood that day; that's all."

"It looked to me like it was more than that. He seemed... drunk."

I let out that last word slowly, making sure to analyze Ali's reaction as I said it to see how he would react. His eyes immediately widened, then he looked from side to side, clearly trying to come up with a story or explanation to get Sandeep out of trouble.

"No, sir, he wasn't drunk. Actually, you see, he got some news that his mother in Pakistan is not well. That got him very upset, hence his behavior that morning. I agree it's not right, but it's understandable, sir. If you too learned your mother was not well and you were so far away, you would also be upset. His mistake was coming to work with his anger when he should have just stayed home."

"So this has never happened before?"

"Never, sir. Sandeep is hard working and always coming early and finishing all his work diligently. This was just one mistake."

That was a lie. I had looked at our cameras and found several similar instances in the past months, all of them with Ali in the store calming Sandeep down and sending him home.

I had given him a chance to come clean, but he kept insisting this was a first-time occurrence and did not warrant any punishment.

All the times Sandeep had showed up drunk, he threatened the staff violently with a wooden stick. How could we tolerate such behavior? How can the staff work and focus when they feel their physical safety is at risk and, on top of that, Ali, their boss, is condoning such behavior by keeping it a secret?

I showed Ali the footage I had gathered, where you could clearly see every instance of Ali taking control of a violent and abusive Sandeep. He was silent.

Whether Sandeep was drunk or not, he was definitely violent and couldn't keep working at Green Leaf. I'd have to let him go and told Ali as much.

As for Ali himself, I suspended him until further notice. I had to speak with the rest of the board to decide what we would do. Ali was a senior member of the team, and I felt like whatever action we took, it had to be with everyone's approval.

At 10:00 p.m. that night, I received a text message from Ali.

"I am resigning effective immediately."

This was unexpected. I was in such shock that Neha instantly knew something terrible had happened.

What a gut punch just before one of our busiest seasons. I knew Ali was furious with me for suspending him and firing Sandeep, but I didn't think he would quit. Here I was about to face a rush of shoppers for the long weekend and our biggest store didn't have any leadership.

Worse, I started to question myself and my decision. Although Ali had clearly shown poor judgment, he was also a key member of the team and excelled in many areas. Was I right in sticking to my guns or should I try and get Ali back to work?

I was also worried other managers would question my judgment and quit in defiance. Ali was experienced and often looked upon as the unofficial leader among the store managers. It was possible they might follow his lead.

The next morning, I was in the office early, asking myself what to do next, when Ali showed up. He wanted to talk to me, and I hoped he had come to apologize.

"Mr. Ram, I have been with Green Leaf for so many years. I was the one who opened the Peninsula branch, I know all our customers, and I was the one who made it the success it is."

This definitely isn't going the way of an apology, I thought.

"All the staff, all the customers, they are loyal to me—not to anyone else. You will see without me, the store will fail and you will fail too. You made a big mistake, and you will regret it."

Those words hit hard, but I knew then and there what had to be done.

"Ali, you resigned on your own. And if you hadn't, I would have had no choice, but to fire you anyway. You are good at your job, but you're not a cultural fit. I wish you the best of luck in your future endeavors. And don't worry about Green Leaf, we will manage."

I was so scared of losing him and the impact it would have on our bottom line, I didn't even stop to think about all the negative impact he had on the store and employee morale. A leader leads by example, and he was setting the wrong one. What he had done went against our values, and no matter how much sales he brought in, he did not fit in with the Green Leaf family.

> **Lesson #3: Don't let fear of failure dictate your decisions.**

I was the leader at Green Leaf and had to make a tough decision, even if it meant rocking the boat and not everyone would agree with it. The timing was terrible, but it only meant I needed to put that much more energy into a transition plan.

> **Lesson #4: Don't assume that colleagues or staff follow blindly.** Once a decision is made, don't second-guess it, but be sure to have a clear rationale that underpins it and explain it to the rest of your team. Being a leader means making tough decisions and sticking to them.

* * *

First things first, I needed to speak with the staff at the Peninsula branch. It needed leadership. I thought I should take over the store temporarily, but what did I really know about handling the day-to-day activities? A few months ago, I didn't know how to bag lettuce properly.

As a leader, you have to learn to delegate and trust people to do the right thing. If you are amazing at sales, you might not be the expert in accounting. You might be the best marketer out there, but perhaps managing Human Resources is not your strength. And even if you are good at everything, there are only so many hours in a day, and those hours should be best spent on your strengths.

So when thinking about the best person to handle the situation, my mind turned to Neema, the current assistant manager of the branch.

I asked her to handle all of Ali's work for the time being and said I was there to fully support her, but she was the best person for the job.

> **Lesson #5: Good leaders do. The best leaders delegate. Don't be afraid to trust those around you, but stick around to give them the proper support to succeed.**

I held a quick meeting with the staff to inform them of Ali's resignation and Neema's new role. I said we needed to get through the busy weekend, and after that, we would see how to move forward. For now, there was no need to dwell on what had happened; it was all on hands on deck.

Next, I spoke to the rest of the management team and explained the situation. I wasn't asking anyone to second-guess my decision; I knew it was the right one. They had the choice to agree or disagree, but as a leader, I needed to ensure everyone heard my rationale.

Over the following days, I spent all my time in the Peninsula branch to help Neema and the rest of the team cope with the extra workload of losing their leader during this busy shopping season. My experience doing odd tasks a few months ago proved invaluable to speed up restocking shelves, help out at the cash machine, or run around to guide customers find the products they needed. I didn't take Ali's place; I let Neema do that. I was an extra pair of hands willing to do anything and everything in the store so no one would feel an extra burden because of a decision I made.

The weekend went without too many hitches, and on Tuesday, we realized the week's sales had gone even better than the previous year. The crisis helped spearhead increased coordination between all the branches so that anyone who had extra stock sent it to the other branch who was running out. The WhatsApp groups sped up communication.

Neema was turning out to be a great choice and a great leader. She knew how to rally not only her team but everyone else at Green Leaf too. She would eventually become permanent in her new role at the branch.

> **Lesson #6: Always stay true to your values. Don't make the false compromise of prioritizing your bottom line over your culture.**

* * *

The same way the conversation with Mrs. Pierrette hit a chord that pushed me to study harder and give it my best, Ali's words hit a nerve.

He was right in a way. I had superficially learned the business and counted on the team to continue executing more or less as is, but with his departure, I realized I didn't need to be afraid of making bigger changes to align ourselves further with our vision.

When you run a business, especially in the early days, you worry about the bottom line. Letting go of an important contributor was not easy, and it engendered many conflicting feelings. In the end though, culture matters more.

If before I was still hesitant to shift things around, I knew now that to decidedly move the company forward, I had to study all our systems and processes in more depth and rethink them.

Ali resigning forced me to make a big decision ahead of a busy week, but I couldn't let future events dictate how things would go for Green Leaf. I had to take control and do the very best I could to improve the company and move us forward.

Mrs. Pierrette would be proud once again.

RAM'S TIPS:

- Don't be afraid of failing, and don't be afraid of giving it your all. We all get challenged beyond our capabilities, but those moments push us to become better than we thought possible.

  - Fear of failure should never dictate your decisions.

- When you hear of inappropriate behavior in your company, trust, but verify.

- Difficult conversations are, by nature, difficult. Find ways to make them easier by choosing a neutral location, for example.

- Being a leader means making some tough decisions. Once a decision is made, don't second-guess, but be sure to have a clear rationale that underpins it and explain that to the rest of your team.

- Entrepreneurs, by nature, like to control and are reluctant to trust. Learn to let go of those instincts and trust those around you.

- Stay true to your values. In the long run, they matter more than your profits.

CHAPTER 11

TRY, TRY, AND
TRY AGAIN

———

Eight months into my stint at Green Leaf, it was time to kick everything into high gear. I needed to find clear ways to increase our sales and improve our profits.

I had gotten lots of ideas from the staff, but it was up to me to prioritize and decide what would have the highest and quickest impact on our bottom line. Our profit before interest and taxes hovered around 10 to 11 percent of sales on average, and I wanted to get this closer to 15 percent. It was a stretch goal, but my philosophy was that you aim for the moon, and even if you miss, you will have reached the stars!

A key component of success for Green Leaf was the fact that we had goods in stock when our competitors did not. The store had been built on complementing our local selection with imports of groceries from Europe, the Middle East, and South Africa primarily. We would buy those ourselves and bring them into the country by sea, air, or road. When Green Leaf was first founded, basics like cereals, milk, and even certain fruits and vegetables all had to be imported; there were no local manufacturers or distributors.

It's hard to fathom but imagine going into your favorite supermarket and finding no corn flakes or ketchup. Would you even shop at such a place? Well, that was the case fifteen years ago in Tanzanian supermarkets before Green Leaf was started.

Of course, things had improved considerably since then, and all the major brands had local distributors covering the basics, but that didn't mean everything was available all the time. Shortages happened when the distributor ran out and had to wait a few weeks or months for their next consignment. Or you could find the basic mayonnaise on the shelf, but what about low-fat or fat-free versions? Customers want choice, but it didn't always make sense for distributors to order those products in large quantities when only a small percentage of the population would be buying them.

Our mission was to offer our customers the best possible product and service in a welcoming, friendly, and fun shopping environment. To offer the range of quality products we aimed for, we had Green Leaf's imports arm.

Based on customer requests or the newest trends we saw in other countries, we sourced products from all over the world. We had gluten-free pasta and kombucha drinks, and we were the first ones to import alternative milks and superfoods.

We knew our customers were tuned to all the latest trends and willing to pay for those. In turn, we were willing to make the effort to find those products, organize and pay all the expensive shipping costs and taxes to Tanzania, and show our customers we had more choices than others did. This was well aligned with our stated vision and mission statement.

The flip side of this operation was that it added to our costs. When we ran out of something and had to bring it by air, it was expensive. A box of corn flakes could end up being priced at $5 on our shelves! This wasn't good for customer satisfaction.

* * *

I discovered another strange thing in the world of international grocery manufacturing and distribution. Take for example your favorite brand of chocolate. You'd think that because it's the same brand, it should taste the same everywhere. Well, you'd be wrong!

Whether it's manufactured in Europe, the United States, South Africa, or in the Middle East, it could all taste slightly, or even sometimes a lot, different. To make sure the food lasts the long travel journey, manufacturers sometimes add preservatives to their original recipes, altering the taste or use different, cheaper raw materials so they could sell their products at a lower price in less developed markets.

For other items like tomatoes, things get even murkier. In his book, *The Empire of Red Gold*, Jean-Baptiste Malet describes how certain less-than-ethical manufacturers abuse the lack of strict food testing and standards in Africa to pass sub-standard products. A can of tomatoes could be made in China, diluted with water or other less appetizing ingredients in Italy, and sold in many countries in Africa as "Made in Italy" products. For that reason, consumers had become very wary of buying food in stores they did not know.[12]

---

12 Jean-Baptiste Malet, *L'Empire de l'Or Rouge: Enquête Mondiale sur la Tomate d'Industrie* (Paris: Fayard, 2017).

Green Leaf was a trustworthy store, and people knew we imported genuine, high-quality products. Our prices were higher than the competition, but it reflected the care we put into sourcing only the best and original items.

I started looking into all the components of our imports business to see if there was room to improve our profitability. It was not an easy task.

First, the Procurement Manager had to take stock of what was in the warehouse, what was about to sell out, and then inform Amir of the products we urgently needed. Based on that list, Amir would go to either Europe, South Africa, or the Middle East for a week-long shopping trip. The bulk of the buying was accomplished by visiting one of the wholesalers with whom we had established a good relationship, which formed 80 percent of the order.

The remaining products came from a variety of small suppliers that had niche products like non-dairy milk or gluten-free snacks. That was a big category for us, expensive to source, but with good margins and a clear differentiator.

Then once the buying was done, funds were wired to confirm the order and the goods arrived at our shipper's warehouse within a few days. We had a shipping agent in each of those countries who would help us consolidate the order and prepare the detailed invoice and documentation for customs.

Once all the paperwork was done and filed at the origin point, the goods were put in a container and sent, while the same paperwork was transmitted to the Tanzanian customs authorities and food inspectors. If sent by sea, you could expect four to six weeks of transit time. By air, things took as little as two days to make their way to Dar airport, but the cost was two-and-a-half times as much, so we only flew in high-value items with a low shelf life—think cheeses, meats, yogurt, and chocolates that need to be kept refrigerated.

Road transport was somewhere in between. It's not easy to drive from Johannesburg to Dar, you had to pass at least two borders with the associated paperwork and delays. Frequently, you had to re-route your trip when one of the checkpoints was too backed up with trucks. And of course, there had to be a road from origin to destination, which meant only goods from South Africa would make it that way. Certainly, nothing from Europe was coming by road!

In operations management, the total time from the beginning of a process to the end is called cycle time, the number of days between when we placed the order from one of our wholesalers to when it arrived at our warehouse in Dar.

By sea, the cycle time averaged ninety days; by road, forty-five days; and by air, we were talking seven days.

Needless to say that in all three scenarios, all this effort took large amounts of time and planning. Because up until now, we didn't have accurate data on our sales per item and category or any way to easily analyze what was running out faster than anticipated and what was slow-moving, we would lose out on sales or have to discount products to sell them before they expired.

Evaluating missed sales was a tough one, but I knew we were losing up to 6 percent of our sales due to discounted or expired products. Now, this also included items damaged in transit and stolen products, but there had to be at least a few percentage profits in there we could save. Some months this could represent more than $60,000.

Lesson #1: To find ways to increase your profitability, start with the easily identifiable problems with quantifiable costs or benefits.

Another issue, paying for these goods up front was a huge use of cash. A normal retailer would sell their products to customers before paying their suppliers, having gotten, on average, thirty days' credit. For our imported goods, we were paying up to 90 days before receiving the products.

Let's take an example with a typical sea shipment from Europe. We imported two containers a month, which means $120,000 in product value. Shipping and insurance were about $10,000, but to do all the paperwork and pay the requisite import duties would cost us another $70,000. We had $200,000 in cash for that shipment alone tied up for three months.

This was money we couldn't use to generate any sales. At that time, our sales averaged $1 million a month, and assuming a 10 percent profit and the fact that typical suppliers gave us thirty days to pay, we were losing out on an additional $300,000 or $3,500 per day.

But that's not the only cost to factor in. The bank charged an average interest rate of 16 percent per year. This means that each day waiting for the goods would cost us an additional $500.

In total, we were losing more than $4,000 each day we waited on this container. That is serious money.

Here is the part I thought was most promising to start saving money. Once our containers arrived at port, it took another week to clear all the customs formalities and get it to our warehouse. There we were dependent on the port authorities and their backlog. Once in our warehouse though, it took our team an average of ten to fifteen days to process all the goods and send them to the stores. This seemed like a long time to me and cost us $40,000 to $60,000 in delays.

Many things were out of our control during the whole process, but this wasn't. How do we make sure we buy the right products and don't run out? Can we reduce the quantity of certain items that never sold at full price? Why was it taking so long to receive the imported items in our warehouse, and how could we accelerate that?

If we could figure out all this, we could save hundreds of thousands of dollars a month. This was huge, and I decided it would be my priority.

* * *

First, we had to proactively look at why we only ordered goods when they ran out. our Procurement Manager, Kabir, didn't always get a good picture of what was selling out from the stores. We fixed that with our IT Manager, Kondo, by providing reports that automatically highlighted when something was sold out in all stores and unavailable in the warehouse. Thanks to the changes we had made earlier in the system, Kabir could have the latest sales information and place orders accordingly.

The next constraint was traveling to those locations. Whenever stock of our imported goods was low, Amir traveled to the relevant location to stock up more. However, those trips had to be scheduled around his availability, and this was one of the main bottlenecks of the import process. It was not always clear when he would make his next trip, so when placing an order for certain products, you weren't sure if you should get three months' worth of sales or six months. Hence, you would lose out on sales or order too much, which ended up expired.

Our initial plan with Nijhad was to let Amir continue doing these trips during the transition period as we figured out an alternative. Amir also had a good sense of food trends and was quick to identify what should be brought over to Dar to keep us ahead of the competition, but now that I was looking at this in more detail, these infrequent trips presented some issues.

By the time we identified a product missing on our shelves, the demand for it had increased, and so we ordered more from the international supplier. We sometimes lost track of whether the same customer was asking for that product or a different one, thus compounding the number of orders and giving us a false picture of demand.

We went from severely understocked to abruptly over-supplied in a matter of months. We now had the system to identify the correct order based on sales, but how could we increase the frequency of deliveries?

Among the 20 percent of small suppliers we were using in Europe, one, Nedstar, kept sending us heavy catalogs and monthly promotions of their full range of items. It seemed they were keen to do more business with us. We usually only bought specialty items from them, like sugar-free biscuits or dairy-free cheeses, that our traditional wholesalers didn't have.

Since we never ordered more from them, I had not initially paid attention to what they supplied until one day I remembered a key lesson from my time in Houston. Our current partners, like the tenants at Kingdom Plaza, were most incentivized to help us succeed and grow. Nedstar fell into this category, so I opened the link in their email and started sifting through their catalog.

Lo and behold, they had a full selection of items that we normally ordered!

We were so used to going the wholesale route that no one ever explored what else was possible. Nedstar, who supplied us all along, could not only get us the full range of items we required but could do so through an online ordering system, which didn't require us to physically go there.

> **Lesson #2: The first place to look for solutions is with your current partners. They are motivated to keep working and even increasing business with you.**

I asked to quickly get a quote on a full container load, and it came up more expensive than we normally paid. I got on the phone with Vanessa, our account manager at Nedstar, and told her our dilemma.

"Hi, Vanessa, this is Ram from Green Leaf. I saw the quote you sent, but unfortunately, it is coming up more expensive than our other suppliers. I would love to work with you, but this is going to sink our margins."

"I'm sorry to hear that. By how much are we talking about, if you can share?"

"Yes, of course, depending on the items, it's coming up to between 5 and 10 percent higher in price. You can imagine that's a lot of our margin eaten up."

"I understand. Let me see what I can do. Could you increase your quantities by any chance? If you buy more, I can get you a better discount."

That was tempting, but if we bought more than our stores could handle, we'd have the same problem of having to discount items before they expired. I had another idea, though, which I thought would work better.

"No, sorry, we know how much we sell, and this is really the best we can do, but there is something else we could try. Could you extend us a thirty-day credit?"

International suppliers didn't typically give credit to foreign firms where they couldn't ascertain their creditworthiness, but we had been doing business with Nedstar for years now. The volume was small, but I hoped our history of paying on time would help our case.

"I need to check with my manager if we can do that. To be honest, it should be possible because we've been working together for so long. Can you send me a copy of your audited reports and latest bank statement? I will see how to push it through."

She kept her word and after speaking with her manager, we got thirty days' credit on up to $40,000, which was more than enough for a container a month, our goal to smooth the inflow of imported goods. This gave meaningful lifeblood to our cash flow!

> **Lesson #3: Improving your cash flow can be as profitable as improving your margins.**

We could still organize Amir's physical trips, but now the stores would not suffer stock-outs in between. And having credit meant we could cut by a third the amount of cash stuck at sea. That cash could be reinvested in getting more products, thus improving our turnover and saving us a lot of interest. I calculated that those extra thirty days minus the additional cost of the goods would benefit us positively by more than $50,000 a month.

And this was before accounting for the impact on lost sales and expired products.

* * *

Now on to the delivery of goods in our warehouse. The first time I witnessed a container truck pulling up in the little alley that served our warehouse, I was both in awe and dismayed.

In awe because when the container doors opened, it felt like Christmas seeing all those products that would soon go on the shelf. Dismayed because the unloading was completely manual. We used to hire twenty to thirty men to spend all day and night unloading the boxes one by one from the truck. Unloading one container took, on average, six hours, and we typically received four containers at a time.

This multi-day process had a cost: the guys we had to hire, the truck drivers, and the cost of the containers themselves that we would be billed for each day they were with us. In addition to the $4,000 per day from above, I estimated we had to pay another $2,000 per day in extra labor and port fees for keeping the containers.

Then in the warehouse, each box of product had to be checked to make sure the item was indeed ordered, the correct quantity was sent, and the expiry dates were reasonable enough for us to sell them in-store. Because of the way the goods were offloaded, the warehouse was a mess, which meant days on end spent trying to retrieve items.

A sample of each item was taken, a sticker put on it with the quantities received, and then given to the manager in charge of entering all that information, including expiry date, into the system.

Each of these processes caused a massive delay, and a small mistake was easily amplified when the manager had to get up and look for a product that could be anywhere in this massive warehouse.

Besides time lost selling the products, we also lost precious days of shelf life for sensitive items. And all that manual handling also meant breakages and damages. There had to be a better way. There was just too much physical labor involved and lack of coordination.

If we could reduce the time spent on offloading by half and save five days from this process, it would be another $30,000 in monthly savings.

I spent weeks in the warehouse looking at all aspects of how goods arrived and were processed. Then I thought of ways to improve the system and spoke with Samir, the Warehouse Manager, to see if it would work. But because getting the goods out in time was so critical, I could only share my ideas during the downtime in the warehouse, once they had processed and sent out all the products. Again and again, Samir found reasons why my ideas would not work.

"What if we organize each room to receive a certain category of items? This room in the warehouse could be for cereal and biscuits, this other one could be for toiletries, and so on."

"No, sir, it won't work because we receive so many of certain items and so little of others. How can we know if we will have enough space for cereals or shampoo just in this or that room?"

After a few weeks, I'd try again.

"What if you took a sample of the item as it gets offloaded from the container? That way Sandra can immediately start the checking and pricing process."

"No, sir, it won't work because if you remove a sample right there and then, you have to open the box, and then you risk breaking the other items, or worse, they are more easily stolen."

Another few weeks passed by.

"What if we use the invoice to check which items are new and which are already in our system? The new items slow down our rate of sending goods to the store because we need to input them first. If we identify them beforehand, then this should go faster."

"No, sir, it won't work because the invoices we get don't have barcodes, so even if we know what is new, we have no way of entering them in the system in advance."

"But wait, Nedstar sends us invoices with barcodes. At least for those shipments, we could pre-enter the information and turn this around faster."

Samir thought about it for a minute.

"Yes, sir, this will work. If we have the barcodes, we can enter it into our system and we could save a day or two in our receiving.

I was making progress! It wasn't as much as I was hoping for, but it was a start.

After almost a year of watching a dozen shipments coming in, I had a eureka moment. I was in London getting a tour of Nedstar's facilities when I saw trucks pull in with goods being delivered. And then I saw the most magical thing happen.

The driver opened the back of the truck, and a Nedstar employee brought a ramp between the truck and the warehouse floor. Another employee then drove a pallet jack (forklift) straight into the truck, picked up a large quantity of goods, and took them straight into the warehouse.

This solution was so simple. It pays to keep your eyes open; you never know when you will learn something relevant to your operations.

> **Lesson #4: It pays to visit your suppliers and partners. You never know which idea you will find that can help your business.**

When I came back to Dar, I shared what I saw with Samir. He was elated, and we got to work right away to figure out how we could adapt this to our situation.

First, we redesigned the warehouse entrance. We created a ramp on the side of the warehouse approximately the height of a container truck, with a gentle slope toward the entrance. And we invested in pallet jacks too. When the goods were loaded at origin, they were put on pallets, but from the beginning of the company's life, when we received only one small container at a time, going manual here in Dar was the best solution.

Despite growing the quantity and frequency of shipments, no one ever rethought the manual offloading process. With a pallet jack and this ramp, we could now easily bring all the goods in a container inside in forty-five minutes, an 88 percent time saving!

Then we reorganized the warehouse to make space in the front so as many of those pallets as possible would fit inside, neatly ordered by category for easy retrieval.

Finally, Kondo also had a great idea to speed up our receiving process. We equipped five of our staff with camera-enabled mobile devices. We downloaded a free app that would allow us to scan a barcode, enter the name of the product, quantity, and expiry date, all in one go. Not only would it remove the bottleneck and massive work the receiving manager had to do, but also upskill the staff.

Our warehouse was significantly better organized, which meant that even if there was a mistake in any data entered, or if Samir wanted to double check an item received, it would take only a few minutes to identify and rectify any issues.

Thanks to a ramp and a few mobile phones, we reduced turnaround time from fifteen days down to four.

Between using Nedstar as a primary supplier and our new and improved warehouse, we saved almost a million dollars in costs annually (a month's worth of sales!). This was incredible and surpassed all my expectations. It also meant we didn't need to sell basic cereals at an exorbitant price. Sometimes all it takes is looking at a problem in a different way and a little perseverance.

RAM'S TIPS:

- When looking to make changes, prioritize your improvements. Where will you get the biggest bang for your buck?

  - Focus on working with your current partners. After all, they have the most to lose if you move your business elsewhere. They can even be a good source of ideas for you!

- Don't be afraid to ask. In negotiations, you don't get what you don't ask for.

- If your first idea fails, try again. Try until you find the idea that sticks.

CHAPTER 12

GETTING INTO THE
MEAT OF THINGS

No, this is not about having to make more changes to our IT system. This chapter is about setting up an actual butchery department in the supermarket.

Green Leaf was oriented toward customers looking for quality products, and we had managed to deliver on almost all fronts. We had high-quality local and imported goods, cheeses, housewares, a coffee shop, and a bakery with pure butter croissants just like those you find in coffee shops in Paris. We were still missing an important category: meats.

We had cured meats (salami, pepperoni, etc.), but we lacked fresh meat. A few local butchers brought us pre-packaged cuts of beef or lamb, but sales were always disappointing and not a single customer was ever satisfied. In fact, when surveying our clients, the number one item they wished we improved on was our fresh meat section.

At that point, Neha and I were pescatarians (we would soon return to eating meat), so it was ironic that I was sitting there wondering how to improve our meat department. Then again, I rarely drink coffee but learned how to make and serve cappuccinos, so I guess it's not that far-fetched!

I discussed this with some of our suppliers and organized visits to their plants. Bad move. What I saw put me off meat even more, and now I was convinced we needed an alternate solution. One of our customers guided me to a butchery in Arusha, in the north of the country, set up there to provide quality cuts to nearby lodges and hotels.

Arusha is a small town, but with a vibrant town center. Still, I wasn't expecting to find so many cars parked in front of this tiny store called The Meat Shop on the Friday morning I visited. It lived by its name! The store must have been no more than fifty square meters but was packed from left to right, and top to bottom, with cuts of meat. Fridges in each corner sold pre-packaged and spiced cuts, and in the back of the store was a large counter displaying bigger cuts ready to be sliced, diced, and minced at a customer's whim. More importantly, the store was filled with people pushing and shoving gently toward the front so they could get what they needed for the weekend. Nervous customers going in not knowing if they'll get what they need, happy customers coming out. That was the sign of a quality operation, overwhelmed with demand.

I met with the owner of the store; a tall woman named Grace. She looked like she was in her mid-forties and had been through hell with her business. Her office was behind the large counter on the side of a cold room so she could monitor the customer flow and what was being taken out of inventory at the same time. As she talked, I quickly understood why her products were in high demand, but she struggled to expand. Typically, it would be for lack of funds, but in her case, she had secured investors and even a line of credit with South African equipment manufacturers. No, her problem was that finding talent and training them was incredibly hard, and theft was rampant.

Margins are tight to begin with. The cost of electricity was almost half of all the expenses. You could never have your cold or freezer room off, so whenever the state utility turned off power, which happened almost every day for several hours, you had to have the generator fueled up and turned on. We were familiar with those challenges. Every time the electricity went off, we lost a batch of breads in the oven.

Fresh meat is also particularly easy to steal. It can easily end up in someone's pocket, or you can under weigh it when selling to a friend. The missing grams add up to lots of money.

No pun intended, but meat was going to be a tough business!

I was hoping Grace would be interested in supplying us in Dar, but she worried that between the costs of running a cold truck for the twelve-hour drive and the high propensity of theft that can happen on the road, it would not be viable. Besides, she had these investor funds and wanted to expand her shop in Arusha. It was doing well, and there was clearly room to do even better.

I was disappointed but not completely hopeless. She put me in touch with her contacts in South Africa where I could investigate what we would need to set up this butchery.

* * *

A few weeks later, I went down to Johannesburg and met with the sales team from King International. They were a large corporation focused on all things food in South Africa. From ovens and fryers to pre-made sauces and spices, if you needed to set up a restaurant, they could do it all and help you run it. And they could do the same for a butchery.

They handed me two catalogs: one for equipment and one for spices and seasonings. Each was over three hundred pages and completely overwhelming. What's the difference between a collagen and cellulose sausage casing? Do I need a thirty-two-inch mincer or a thirty-four-inch one? What's a bandsaw? And all these questions before even opening the second catalog!

> **Lesson #1: If you don't know something, don't hesitate to get outside expertise. Even if it costs money, it will be more than made up by the number of hours saved trying to read and learn on your own.**

I couldn't do this alone. I needed help, but where to start? I searched on Google to see if any food consultancies could help. There were none. Then I remembered something. Back in my early investing days when I was a generalist, every time we looked at an industry we didn't know or understand, we would find an ex-executive from one of the large companies who was doing consulting work. He or she would gladly spend a few hours on the phone or meet us to explain the ins and outs of whatever industry we were researching.

I just needed to find someone who maybe was a butcher or owned a butchery and could help decipher the lingo. Luckily, I was in South Africa, a country well-known for the quality of its meats and braai (barbeque). Except braai is not only something you do on a Sunday with friends and family. Here, it's an any-day, any-time passion!

I found a few people on LinkedIn who seemed to fit the profile, and I reached out.

Hello,

I am the owner of a supermarket chain in Tanzania, East Africa. We are looking to set up a butchery department and want help to do so. I am in Johannesburg this week and was wondering if you had time to meet and discuss a consulting opportunity. Please let me know—thanks!

Regards,
Ram

I must have sent fifteen messages, but returned to Dar empty-handed or, rather, with two heavy undecipherable catalogs.

Another week passed by when Arnold, one of the contacts I had made, replied. He didn't look at his LinkedIn very often but saw my message and would love to meet if it wasn't too late. I had left Johannesburg, but we agreed to discuss my requirements over the phone.

Three weeks later, he flew to Dar es Salaam. Little did I know we would become friends over the next few years, but when I first saw him exiting the airport secure area, I was a bit scared. Arnold is an Afrikaner, a Southern African ethnic group descended from predominantly Dutch settlers that first arrived there in the seventeenth and eighteenth centuries. He is a bit over six feet, towering well above me, about twice my width, with a long Santa Claus beard, and when he spoke English, you feared he was angry at you.

"Hi, Arnold! Welcome to Tanzania!" I said recognizing him from his LinkedIn profile photo.

"Eeesh, that was the worst flight of my life. I can't believe they still make planes this small," he replied.

Afrikaners are known to be direct people; they cut through all the niceties and just want to get the work done.

If I thought I had cultural shock moving from New York to Dar, Arnold would be in for some fun times too.

Over the course of four days, we toured the stores, the competition, the supply chain, and he even looked at the catalogs I brought back from King. He laughed when I showed them to him. Of course, he had seen them before, but he knew all the equipment he needed by heart and didn't need any reference guide.

What seemed like a direct and harsh exterior translated into someone flexible and willing to work with our scant resources. He was a people person at heart and everyone, me included, found his directness charming. When he complained about the flight, he wasn't annoyed at anyone, but he wouldn't sugarcoat anything either. Once he said what he had to say, the matter was over in his mind. With Arnold, you always know where you stand, and even when he's annoyed at you, you're always on his good side.

> **Lesson #2: Find honest partners who can tell you how things really are, and are willing to work within your means and resources to find a solution.**

He quickly assessed the situation, and it was bad.

"Listen, Ram, I have to be honest with you."

Oh no! I thought. *Over the few days I've known him, I didn't see him be anything but honest. It can't be good if he has to be extra honest!*

"I don't think you'll get the quality of meats you want with the suppliers you have currently. I don't want to alarm you, but the standards are not *lekker.*"

Lekker is an Afrikaans word that means good. I would come to learn a few Afrikaans words from Arnold.

He continued, "The only good news here is that your customers seem to know it's the fault of the suppliers and not you. So if you want to continue with them, it's fine."

"What if we wanted to do better? What would it take?"

"*Ag*, that's going to be a lot of work!"

Ag is the equivalent in Afrikaans of "Oh man."

"We're going to have to first find better quality meat. I don't know yet where that could be, but I got some hints from someone at the Namibian embassy that a farmer had pretty good quality meat. Then we'll need the right equipment. I see you have those catalogs, but most of the things in there are rubbish. You only need four pieces of equipment to set up a proper butchery. And, finally, you'll need to find and train good staff. You need a good head butcher and for that, I have some leads. Then we can see who in the supermarket wants to be trained up; that way you'll save on hiring costs, but it's going to be a lot of work, so you better be ready for this."

This was a lot to unpack.

- We had a full schedule and other than at breakfast or before dinner, he had no time to himself. Where did he meet anyone from the Namibian embassy?

- It was good that we needed very little new equipment!

- What leads could he have on a head butcher? I spent the entire time with him and didn't get any leads.

- Minimizing hiring and focusing on training our staff was a good idea. I always liked to give opportunities to our staff first.

After some discussions with Nijhad, we decided the effort was worth the risk and investment. Looking at our vision, we needed to have a solid butchery as part of our offering inside the supermarket. It would be tedious to set all this up and get it right, but I hadn't seen anyone so resourceful and adaptable as Arnold. I thought that if we had a shot at making something special, it would be with him.

* * *

We started by ordering the pieces of equipment we needed: a mincer, a bandsaw, a sausage maker, a patty press, along with a few specialized knives and tables.

Between manufacturing and import delays, it would take three months for the equipment to arrive. Arnold focused on getting the bare minimum because he understood something important: customers had lost trust in buying meat in Dar. Even if we got everything right, it would not be easy to convince them of what we had, so better to start with a small investment and grow from there. That's my kind of thinking.

> **Lesson #3: When starting a new department, consider whether you can start small to test it out with your customers. That way if you see no traction, you wouldn't have spent too much time or money.**

Next was finding the meat. Using his Namibian contact, we found the farmer whose meat was prized by the embassy. Robert is a Tanzanian man in his mid-thirties, originally from the north of the country, but he relocated close to Dar to run his farm. He was passionate about farming and working for himself.

When he was eighteen, he met a South African farmer in Tanzania and, looking for a job, joined him to help with the cattle. He spent five years working day and night learning the trade. One day, he met a Kenyan farmer working just across the border. Keen to learn from a fellow East African, he joined up and worked between Tanzania and Kenya for another five years until he felt confident that he knew enough about the best of both farming worlds. Through his first employer, he got a few cows for free and had been breeding them ever since.

Arnold thought that Robert's skills were rough, but he was excited to learn. The breed of beef was also rare, imported originally from South Africa, but which had developed some unique Tanzanian qualities due to the differing climate and feed. The Namibians liked it so much because it was close enough to their taste, but with a local twist!

Throughout this time, I also got to know more about Arnold's background. After serving in the military in his youth, he ended up in the butchering business, but funnily enough, couldn't quite remember how. He had worked in Scotland and the United States, where he got to see how people work with meat, which is why he was so flexible. He had seen other ways of making it work with scant resources.

I spent a day on Robert's farm, but Arnold insisted on spending a full week there. The brief to Robert was simple: he needed to supply us meat only from grass-fed cows that had been slaughtered before they hit two years old. Arnold gave him more tips on how to take care of his herd and how to slaughter properly.

Note to Self #1: Sometimes you learn about things you never knew you would care about. Sweating the small stuff can really take you in many directions!

Afrikaners have farmer roots, and I suspect Arnold enjoyed spending time there. He came back refreshed, but we had another problem. For the quantities we needed even as a start, Robert could not supply us in full. He could build his cattle, but he would need a cold truck to deliver the quantities we needed weekly. He also needed more investment to pay other farmers to allow his cows to graze on their grass. This was all money he didn't have and we weren't ready to make an investment in his business. We set the problem aside for now, at least we knew the quality was there.

It would take some time for Robert to supply us with the exact quality we wanted, but we still could get started with his meat. The quality was superior to anything else we found, and it would only improve over time.

On to the next big challenge! Arnold said he had potentially found a head butcher, but that person already had a job at a competing supermarket. We went to see how his meat cuts were and came back disappointed. Regardless of the meat quality, a good butcher needs to have a good handle on their knife (pun intended) and produce consistent cuts. This was not the case.

I didn't know anyone in the meat business except Grace, so I phoned her and asked for advice. The only other way to find a talented butcher, she said, was to try all the small local butchery shops and see if there's any raw talent (another pun!). This was a very long shot; dozens of shops were in and around the peninsula area where our main store was, and none even had refrigerators to keep their meat from sweltering in the pervasive Dar heat. Nevertheless, I had no other option at this stage, so Arnold and I went around meat shops all across the city.

These stores are not on any map apps or review sites. They are often not on the main roads either. They are at almost every corner, tucked between an airtime vendor and a *duka* (small shop) selling biscuits and cigarettes. We must have walked into at least twenty of them over three days, and avoided even more because of the smell, but on the fourth day, we got a break. The shop was not particularly better than the other ones we visited, but the owner had a brother who used to work in Uganda in a supermarket butchery. He had just returned to be closer to his wife and kids and was looking for a job.

We met Musa the next day, and Arnold put him to work. I wasn't qualified to judge knife skills, but Musa had a quality I instantly recognized: leadership. Once given control of the area, he owned his workspace. He immediately got to work, no questions asked, and started serving customers. He understood what they were looking for and did everything with a smile. It makes a big difference to the confidence your customers have in your store when they see the attendants are attentive. I hoped his knife skills were as sharp as his smile, then we would have a winner.

A few hours later, Arnold told me his knife skills were great. It would need some fine-tuning once Robert's meat arrived because of the difference in quality, but the talent was there. More importantly, Musa also had passion. He just stayed there the whole day working, not knowing if he would get the job or even get paid. He enjoyed so much being at the store, cutting meat and helping customers. That's what we look for in our staff. More than even talent, you need to have a passion for helping customers. We hired him on the spot and paid him for his interview day as well. Musa was over the moon.

> **Lesson #4: The best interviews are when people can be tested live for their job skills.**

* * *

I had been thinking about how we could help Robert with his financial situation. He had everything we were looking for and his meats would be a key component of our section; we had to find a way. With the recent changes we had made on the imports process, we started saving quite a bit of money and working capital. We didn't have the cash to invest in his business, but maybe we could advance him the funds to operate. In essence, instead of paying thirty days after delivery, we would give him a big advance now and deduct it from each of his deliveries.

With that cash upfront and a secure contract with us, we could together go to the bank and help him get a loan. That was a clever way of using the limited resources we each had, but also building on the relationships the supermarket had relied on all this time. Robert was extremely thankful for the opportunity. Our sales were so brisk that we recovered our advance from him in less than a year.

In the same way, I tried to learn about our bakery business, I spent a week learning about the meat business. You don't have to wake up as early, but this work was more physical. Even with all the machines, it's hard work cutting up the meats with the bandsaw. The mincer required pulling kilos of meat back and forth until it's finely done. Then the sausage filler needed a quick operation of the hands every few seconds to get just the right length of sausage. Not to mention hanging the meat in one place or another until it dries properly, weighing it to check it lost enough moisture, vacuum packing large cuts, and then whenever customers need smaller cuts, opening up the bags and cutting them just right. There were burgers to be made and kebabs to be spiced and marinated with exact recipes provided by Arnold. He was a tough instructor who was kind when teaching, but strict if you didn't follow what he was doing. The room where we worked was cold—no sweating was happening here!

Finally, D-Day was upon us. Almost six months after my first call with Arnold, we were ready to open the butchery section.

I was very nervous. I knew it would be an uphill battle, but I was confident that we were delivering a unique experience in Tanzania. Looking at the display that morning, I could see we had created magic. We had ribs, T-bones, steaks, burgers, and sausages made with chicken, lamb, beef, and pork. We also had marinated chicken and beef cut in cubes and ready to be grilled in the oven or in a barbecue. With Arnold's help, we created recipe flyers for customers to grill, fry, bake, or roast meat whichever way they wanted so they knew exact cooking times for what they were buying.

We didn't advertise the section, figuring we could learn from customers what they liked and slowly adjust our production. Everything kept selling out. The word-of-mouth spread so fast we couldn't keep up! Customers who never shopped with us because they thought we were too expensive now came just for the butchery section.

This was a big success, more than we could even imagine. Most of what we accomplished so far with Green Leaf was in the background. This was the first time customers could see real change happening in the store, and they loved it. They loved that we listened to them, that we tried, and that we were succeeding in providing a quality offering. The vision of Green Leaf becoming a full-service, high-quality grocer was finally coming to fruition.

RAM'S TIPS:

- If you're setting up a new department or division, learn from others who have already gone through the process. If necessary, hire consultants or advisors. This will greatly accelerate your learning and prevent you from making easily avoidable mistakes.

    - External advisors can also help improve an existing department and bring you best practices or innovative problem-solving techniques.

    - Make sure those advisors understand your business model and can work within your constraints. Interview them like you were going to hire them!

- If someone says it can't be done, understand why first and see if you can challenge those assumptions. Sometimes it requires creative problem-solving.

- If you're starting something new that you're unsure about, think about starting small to minimize the money spent and effort expended.

- When interviewing, see if you can test the candidate live for their job skills.

CHAPTER 13

YOU CAN'T BUY TRUST

———

Accounting was a boring subject. I always found it to be a staid version of finance. Maybe the cousin from the more serious-minded side of the family: always trying to get the numbers right, unadventurous, quietly doing work in the background just so finance could come in with its fancy tools to actually return you cash above and beyond your wildest dreams.

It's no wonder, then, that one of the last areas left to revamp was the Accounting department. It would also prove the most tedious.

Balendra was in charge and he had been there for almost ten years. The only issue was that Balendra didn't have a formal degree in accounting; he was self-taught. It was not a problem in and of itself, but the issue was what he focused on learning.

Amir, like most entrepreneurs of his generation, was focused on the cash in and out. His success was based solely on one metric: his bank balance. However, cash in the bank does not always reflect the true nature of the business. It hides what you owe your suppliers, what loans you've taken from the bank. It can't even really tell you whether you're profitable or not.

For a business the size of Green Leaf, we needed to switch to accrual accounting. This meant measuring our sales against our purchases and figuring out which products we were making money on. We needed to move from intuition to hard facts, and we could only do so with the proper system and a new mindset from the Accounting team.

As I had learned in Financial Reporting & Control in business school, three main statements show the financial health of a company: income statement, balance sheet, and cash flow statement.[13]

- The income statement shows the profit and loss made.

- The balance sheet shows the assets and liabilities a company has. An asset can be cash in the bank, inventory on the shelves, or equipment in the factory. Liabilities are what you owe others, typically the bank and suppliers. The difference between assets and liabilities, hopefully positive, is called equity, which is what the company is worth.

- Finally, the cash flow statement shows how changes in the income statement and balance sheet impact the cash the company has in the bank.

Without using such a system, we could not tell if the products we sold in the bakery were profitable. Which supplier sold us cans of tuna that made us more money, both in terms of margins and absolute amount? Should we really be selling homeware?

---

13 V.G. Narayanan, "Financial Reporting and Control" (lecture, Harvard Business School, Boston, MA, Fall 2009).

I couldn't answer any of those questions, but I was determined to remedy this.

If it sounds esoteric, it's because I believe accounting was invented by people who wanted to make business sound like rocket science. In fact, it's not complicated, but the terminology is hard to remember unless you're versed in it day and night.

For our task on hand though, the main point to remember is this: your assets should equal the sum of your liabilities and equity. And in the case of Green Leaf, it didn't. Or let me rephrase, it did once a year when we did a full inventory check. At that point, we counted every single product on the shelf in all our stores and warehouse simultaneously. It was a tedious and excruciating process but needed to be done.

Inventory is categorized as an asset as per the powers that be of accounting, but if not handled correctly, it can also be a huge liability.

Let me explain. For a retail business, inventory is the source of cash, but it can also be a loss of cash. The simplest example is a clothing store. If you owned a small clothing store and you bought clothes that were in season, you would sell those clothes quickly and make a nifty profit. If, on the other hand, you bought clothes that no one in their right mind would wear, then you would have spent all your money and not make a single dime off those clothes. Your inventory could have been a source of cash but was instead a complete loss.

Your inventory can also be stolen, damaged, or broken. For a grocery business, all food items are perishable and if not sold by the best before date, it's as good as money lost. You can imagine how right we have to be to buy certain fresh items like fruits and vegetables or meats that have a short shelf life. In less than seven days, if not sold, you have to throw them out. And how easy it is for staff or customers to steal small bottles of liquor, easy to hide and high in value.

Well, at Green Leaf, with the way the system was designed at the time, we needed to trust all staff and customers completely. Since we were doing our inventory check only once a year, any theft would not be found until then. Even if wrongly entering the quantity of items received was an innocent mistake, we wouldn't find that out either until the big inventory check.

I'm all about trust, but verifying occasionally that the trust is justified is a good idea.

* * *

Our system was the issue. Green Leaf switched to an advanced inventory and financial system a few years prior, an Enterprise Resource Planning software (or ERP in tech parlance), but it had not been implemented fully or tested. It could do so much, but without proper implementation, it was no better than a spreadsheet. Actually, it was worse because it could even give you false or misleading results. It was like having spent the money on a Ferrari but finding it was going too fast, you replace the engine with that of a Lada.

We had already cleaned up the inventory database with products that were being sold and categorized them properly. So first, we needed to know what was on our shelf and what was showing up on our system. This was not standard Green Leaf practice, but we decided to do a mid-year stock count. Three intense nights of checking and rechecking gave us an accurate picture of what we owned.

We checked those figures against the system, and the results were appalling. Horrifying, frightening, petrifying, alarming. Pick your most panicked sounding feeling! We had a 75 percent discrepancy rate, meaning we were missing 75 percent of the items we thought we had!

This was serious. Nijhad and I had bought this business assuming enough inventory was for sale. You could see it on the shelf, but now the system was showing that three-fourths were missing. Were we lied to? Were we so naive to have missed this completely?

I called Nijhad to check what he thought about this.

"Hey, man, I have some disturbing news. We just did the inventory count, and it looks like we're missing 75 percent of the stock."

"What?! That's impossible; it doesn't make any sense. We've been running this business for so many months now and haven't had any issues of stock so far. How is this even possible?"

"I don't know; it doesn't make sense to me either. I can't explain it."

"So how much value are we talking about here?"

"I'm not sure; I only checked the quantity of items. Let me check how much that represents in shillings and I'll call you back."

I pulled up my spreadsheet and added another column showing the cost of every single item. Multiplying it by the quantity columns from the system and the physical count would yield me the value of the inventory. The difference was staggering; the system was telling us we should have had $8 million of inventory, but the physical count was only showing $2 million.

My heart skipped a beat. Actually, it felt more like six million beats. I felt scared. For the first time since the lettuce-bagging incident, I thought I had made a big mistake moving to Dar and buying this business. Even during the whole Ali episode, I had never felt so close to just giving it all up and going home.

I called Nijhad and told him the result, fully expecting to hear anxiety on the other end of the line. I could hear him on the phone clicking and typing away but, suddenly, a sigh of relief.

"So, what do you think?"

"We're fine, Ram; there's nothing to worry about."

"What do you mean?" My voice was as panicked as his was relieved.

"I'm not sure what the system is showing, but when we looked at the books from back when we did the acquisition, that's approximately the same amount of inventory we had seen. We're fine. We just need to figure out what's wrong with this system."

Everything! Everything was wrong with this system!

As I felt a sigh of relief from what Nijhad said, I felt another wave of panic. How on earth would we fix something that was so off. The investment had been hefty. We couldn't afford to switch to a new system, both in terms of cost and implementation time.

We couldn't revert to the old system either. Not only had it not been in use for two years and missing critical information, but it was also woefully inadequate for managing the four stores we had. And forget being able to handle our growth plans.

I had lunch with Neha that day, and she could clearly see I was in one of those moods. She asked me what happened, and I told her the whole story and how dejected I felt. She did not seem nearly as concerned though, and I asked her why.

"Well, you already knew you were here to make changes, and this system is just another problem to fix. It shouldn't come as a surprise that it's a mess."

"Yes, I know, but it just feels like nothing is working right. Without a system, how are we supposed to improve this business? We need data to understand what's going on. It's been the whole issue since the beginning."

"You're only partly right, honey. Yes, data is critical, but think about it; you just had more than half your team work every night for the past three nights to count and re-count all the stock in the stores, something they had not done in who knows how long. And they did it because you asked them. Without complaints, they worked all night alongside you because you explained to them why it was important to do so. That's a long way from where you first started, don't you think?"

That was true. I had let myself get overwhelmed by this situation and took for granted what had just happened. I led the team and they followed. The results were less important than the process at this point. And if we had gotten this far, I knew exactly where to turn to figure out how we could fix this: the team again.

Lesson #1: If your team is strong and your leadership good, you can surmount any problems.

I gathered Balendra from Accounts, Neema from our Peninsula store, and Kondo from our IT department. They were instrumental in getting this stock count done and would be instrumental in brainstorming a solution.

We discussed the problem at length. Frankly, no one was surprised the system was so off. It had been implemented with all the wrong data from the beginning, so that initial mistake had just been growing. As we saw it, we already had fixed one of the main issues; we had gathered the correct inventory data thanks to our stock count.

Now the bigger problem. We needed to finish the implementation of the system. As it turns out, the software we used to record sales at the cash machine was not communicating directly with the ERP. A manual upload/download had to be done every week to update the sales figures.

In addition, because the coding had not been thoroughly tested, it looked like if a customer bought a pack of four milk cartons that were sold together, only one unit of milk was deducted from the inventory. Sometimes the opposite problem would happen, where a customer bought one can of soup, but multiple were deducted.

Did I say thoroughly tested? It didn't look like it had been tested at all!

Lesson #2: When implementing new software, make sure to thoroughly test it.

Normally, these mistakes would have been caught during an extensive testing period. To save money, the previous management decided to forego testing entirely, and the contract with the IT firm that implemented the software didn't include any maintenance. Kondo made many pleas for some funding to clean up these issues, but it was deemed unnecessary and the issues were left to fester.

Now was the time to rectify this. We brought back the IT firm and gave them the run-down of all the issues we were facing. They were supportive and even willing to do it at a reasonable price, but they wanted to also give me a demo of the full capabilities of the ERP.

It was used all over the world by small and medium companies, and many retailers our size and bigger. The reporting tools looked phenomenal. We should have been able to see sales by category, by product, and by time it was sold the moment the sale happened. With proper input, we could see the exact margins we were making on each item, how much was sold and bought, what had expired, or which products were damaged. All these reports were easy to create and user-friendly. Heck, it could be sent automatically to whoever needed it as frequently as required. There was just one caveat; it needed good data. And good data required buy-in from the team. And buy-in from the team required trust.

* * *

Trust was hard. Imagine admitting every day to the system that you overbought bananas and half of them were going bad. Or that you forgot to order butter in bulk for the bakery and gave them the store stock instead, which was almost double the price. Those are not things you want to admit to your boss. All this time you hoped those small mistakes would go unnoticed because you still did your job well. And if you didn't know there was a better way, you would simply think this was part of your job. Sometimes customers buy fewer bananas and more bread, but you can't predict that? Or can you?

Indeed, it's difficult to predict, but if you had all the sales information for every single day for the past decade, it would be much easier to do so. It was all there, but no one could see it, let alone use it.

We learned in business school that leading change is one of the hardest things you can do. It requires vision, alignment, and motivation. For the change process to be effective, it needs eight steps:[14]

---

14 John P. Kotter, "Leading Change: Why Transformation Efforts Fail," *Harvard Business Review,* May-June 1995.

1. Establish a sense of urgency

2. Form a powerful guiding coalition

3. Create a vision

4. Communicate the vision

5. Empower others to act on the vision

6. Plan for and create short-term wins

7. Consolidate improvements and produce still more change

8. Institutionalize new approaches

To start on this path, it was time for another executive meeting. If the last one was about communication and letting go of the past, this time it was about potential and opportunities for the future. For what could be. I showed them the demo of the information we could have and all the reports the system could generate. I told them the one thing it required: they and their teams needed to trust management that this data wouldn't be used against them.

I got blank stares all around. I had been convincing right until that point. The culture had always been one of hiding your mistakes for fear of it being used against you. Control was centralized. There were no objective ways to measure performance for each staff member; it was all at the whim of senior management. Changing habits on the system would require first implementing an even more drastic change—a fair and objective review system for all the staff.

Together with Balendra (who also managed HR along with Accounts), we created detailed job descriptions and review sheets for every position in the company. The exercise was tedious and took weeks to compile. Once done, we held sessions with all managers so they could understand how they would be scored and how to score their team. I can't remember how many times I used the words *fair* and *objective*, but it had to be at least a dozen times a day for a week straight.

It worked because it came from me, the guy who wore a badge just like everyone else, spent early mornings in the bakery, helped close the shop at night, and worked multiple nights to do the stock count. I had no ego and had shown it. They believed me. More importantly, they believed in me.

Lesson #3: Trust helps you lead.

After a few weeks of doing this exercise and compiling the results, we had it. The first official staff review for the entire company. This was mid-year and well understood no compensation would come from this, but it gave everyone a baseline for the end of year review. And it built the trust needed to push the bigger change to the system.

In the back end, we made all the changes necessary to maximize the time spent by the IT firm, but in the front end, we rolled out the changes very slowly, training the staff on each modification we did by carefully and methodically explaining how critical it was to enter the information right.

People got it. Now their review and compensation were not tied to their manager's whim but to entering data accurately and without fail. I thought this change would be hard to digest, but most of the staff were proud of the additional responsibilities. For those who had never used a computer, it was a way to upskill. For others who had been with Green Leaf for a long time, they finally understood what sold and what didn't. Adding it as part of their review emphasized that their view was taken seriously by management.

After just a week of entering this information, the first reports came out. And the results were staggering. Shocking, astonishing, stupefying, amazing. We were seeing weekly sales as soon as the week was closed. Not only that, we finally had a clear picture of how much was sold of each item on any given day. And we could see how much of certain products we were throwing away as a result of over-buying. We could even understand the consumption of ingredients from the bakery.

I knew the company was profitable, but I didn't understand why. This was telling me why. Certain categories of products were outshining others and bringing in much better profits. The margins on all our houseware items—things like plates, bowls, kitchen gadgets—were almost double that of grocery, but we could also tell the stock had been sitting there for months, which meant the inventory wasn't turning nearly as fast as milk, an item ordered multiple times a week, but with a tiny profit margin.

Most surprising was the pet food. Here was a category I never paid much attention to until I saw the numbers in the report.

We imported most of it ourselves, which made the product expensive. Because it wasn't an area of focus, we put a higher margin than our regular groceries. Yet we sold out almost regularly of all basic dog and cat food. We couldn't get enough, and the staff on the ground confirmed it. In fact, the attendant in charge of the pet food department suggested we should order double the quantity and raise the price another 15 percent because the items were selling too fast!

In addition, armed with this detailed sales information, we could now order almost exactly the quantities we required of each product week by week. We could order enough fruits on a Friday that we knew would last us until we received our next order on Monday, without worrying that we would run out of something or have to put something else on special. That visibility alone, reducing our wastage of expired products, helped us improve margins by another point.

To keep this up, we now had to make one last change to our process, and it had to do with stock counts. We couldn't just do it once a year and hope there was no theft because everyone around us was honest. We knew some bad apples were in the company, and thieves often came in the store pretending to be customers but trying to steal whatever they could.

This was such a tedious exercise though! We took three nights to do this last one, and I was exhausted. I couldn't imagine doing it regularly, let alone put a team on it every few months.

Here, Kondo and Neema came up with an elegant solution. We already had a sense of the products that had the most discrepancies in inventory: alcohol, tobacco, and baby food. These were the most likely to get stolen, and from the looks of it, people had served themselves plenty over the years.

They came up with the idea of picking a list of no more than one hundred items that would be checked daily by the store manager before the opening. This was not too overwhelming a list, could be done in less than thirty minutes, and gave them the tools to identify any discrepancy early on.

Within a month of implementing this, we caught one staff member and two "customers" serving themselves from our shelves. As soon as a discrepancy was noted the next morning, our security staff looked at the camera footage from the prior day. With only one zone to focus on, we could easily identify what happened and who was responsible. There were quite a few mistakes in counting, don't get me wrong, but once the first thief was apprehended, everyone took this counting to the next level. It's sad to find out a staff member you trusted is stealing from you, but the rest of the team was even more disappointed in their colleague.

This served as a powerful pressure system among the staff to keep everyone honest. I am not naive, and I know theft was still happening. You can implement all the security and processes you want; people will find a way to get around them, but now I was armed with two powerful countermeasures—the right tools for the managers and the trust of my staff.

We now had a world-class system fully installed and ready to go, along with a team motivated and inspired. Don't let anyone ever tell you accounting is too difficult to understand. You never know what it might reveal if only you pay attention to it.

In the last year, we had clarified our vision and mission statement, provided uniforms to all the staff to revamp our image, improved our ordering, upgraded our ERP system, enhanced our accounting, and, most of all, boosted morale. Green Leaf had prided itself on being at the forefront of the Tanzanian market when it came to the variety and quality of goods it carried and its customer service. Now it could also pride itself on the way it managed its staff and ran its operations.

I had built more legitimacy into the role thanks to a clear vision, actions that were consistent with the company's values, and putting the interest of the company above all.

We had built Green Leaf's team and systems for scale, and it was time for more.

RAM'S TIPS:

- Learn what the three financial statements (income statement, balance sheet, cash flow statement) can tell you about your business.

- Remember the importance of working capital. There's a difference between being profitable (making money on paper) and being solvent (having the cash to pay your staff and suppliers).

- If you're changing a system, process, or software, test it first on a small scale before implementing it.

- For a change process to be effective, follow these eight steps:

  - Establish a sense of urgency

  - Form a powerful guiding coalition

  - Create a vision

  - Communicate the vision

  - Empower others to act on the vision

  - Plan for and create short-term wins

  - Consolidate improvements and produce still more change

  - Institutionalize new approaches

- Connect the dots: inventory checks led to performance management roll-out!

- Trust bridges the gap between being an effective manager and becoming a successful leader.

CHAPTER 14

EXPECT THE UNEXPECTED

———

I developed a routine to ensure I spent enough time in each of our stores.

Every morning before breakfast, I would check the previous days' sales for each store. If we had introduced a new product or ran a new promotion, I was keen to see how they were doing, but in general, I used those reports to give me a sense of what had moved the previous day and prepare questions for the staff.

After a quick breakfast, I headed to the Peninsula store, which was five minutes from our home and had a coffee shop inside. I would order tea, keep pouring over the sales or whatever preoccupied me that day, and looked around the shop to see the first customers coming in.

> **Lesson #1: Spend time where your business is actually happening. It's hard to know what is going on otherwise.**

Another advantage of spending time in the stores: it allowed the staff to come and talk to me. Often, they asked questions about our specialty products.

"What is the difference between red and white quinoa?"

Answer: "No real difference."

"What is cauliflower rice?"

Answer: "It's made out of cauliflower and a low-carb substitute for those on special diets."

"Why are chia seeds so small but so expensive?"

Answer: "They're expensive to grow and imported from South America, but I might have found a farm locally that started producing them, so we'll get a cheaper solution soon!"

Sometimes the staff would ask about an issue they're facing ("we always run out of such and such product and must get more") or convey feelings from a customer ("we need to get vegan sausages" or "our mangoes are not good quality").

The most interesting conversations for me were when we talked about local politics. I read the news in English, but the Swahili one sometimes gave a different perspective.

And of course, rumors were always going around that no newspaper would print, but that would give a sense of the latest government thinking.

One morning I heard the rumor that the government was short of money and had told each ministry they had to figure out for themselves how they could increase their revenues to pay their staff.

Revenues for them meant tax collections for our business. Or worse.

We needed at least a dozen government licenses to operate and displayed all of them prominently on a wall at the entrance of the supermarket along with a photo of the current president.

We had a business license to operate, a VAT license for value-added taxes, a butchery license to cut and process meat, a bakery license for making bread, a packaging license to pack the bread and sell it in plastic bags, a liquor license to sell alcohol, even a music license to play tunes inside the store! We were compliant with all the ministries we could think of, but you never knew what regulations had just come up that were in some way applicable to us.

So on that Wednesday, while I was grabbing my morning tea at the store, I knew there was trouble when I saw a dozen official-looking men along with three armed guards enter the supermarket.

Neema went to greet them; meanwhile, I called our company lawyer and told him to come to the store immediately.

These gentlemen were from the Ministry of Health, and someone had "tipped" them that we were selling expired products.

Of course, this wasn't true, but they insisted on checking every single aisle.

Despite the menacing entry, they were mostly friendly—until they came to the tinned goods section and found a few cans of tomatoes with slight dents on them.

A customer or staff member could have knocked over the cans and caused the dents, but it didn't make a difference. We were fined for selling goods "unfit for consumption" and now had to pay $5,000 for each dent, $25,000 in total within seven days.

Even more concerning, they wanted to shut down the store immediately and had brought chains and padlocks to do so.

Neema and I both pleaded with the officers, but to no avail. There was no stopping them, and I had no idea what we were going to do.

Just then, our lawyer arrived and started talking to them as well, asking in a polite but firm way to see the regulations governing such a huge fine.

They were speaking fast in Swahili, and I couldn't understand everything they were saying. One moment there were grave faces all around, then an astonished look, multiple vigorous hand gestures, and finally, smiles.

From then on, the officers ignored all of us except our lawyer, who they kept talking to, alternating between smiles and looks of consternation.

I knew Neema understood the situation, but I was too worried to ask her there and then what was going on, preferring to let the professionals handle it.

After another twenty minutes of chatting near the bakery, the officers left.

It turned out that our lawyer was from the same village as one of the senior officers, and they had family in common. The looks of consternation were from updates on each member of their families and any elders who had passed away.

Thanks to his family bonds, he convinced the officers to reduce our fine to a more reasonable $5,000, lumping all the dents into one, and our promise that we wouldn't sell unfit foods anymore so they wouldn't close the store.

We got lucky that day. If our lawyer had not been so quick to arrive or had been from another part of the country, the store could have been shut for who knows how long.

I had joined various business groups, and most owners reported an increase in such inspections. They felt more like harassments, to be honest.

There is a tendency to think the laws aren't clear when you work in emerging markets, but it's the contrary. There are strong laws in place with written rules and regulations.

However, the enforcement is left to local officials who might have different agendas.

It's important to have a thorough understanding of those laws and ensure you steer clear of any issues.

After this close call, Nijhad and I decided to hire a few more specialists to guide us through what we didn't know and train our staff on what to look out for. No more would we be caught with damaged cans or packaging with faded labels.

Lesson #2: If you're prepared, you don't need to be lucky to surmount a difficult situation.

* * *

One area of concern was from the Ministry of Labor, who kept a hawk eye on all expatriates working in the country and their visa status.

Because of the long process to get work permits, we would often get business visas for staff and have them start work while the paperwork was ongoing. We had checked this in the past, and this was perfectly acceptable as per current regulations.

Thanks to our hired consultants, we knew on the spot when those regulations changed and decided that the two staff we had in this situation were better kept at home, salary paid, but not doing anything until we cleared their visas.

Such rapid changes in regulation had a non-negligible impact on our cost of doing business and profitability.

They also challenged our values. When the officers threatened to shut down our store, what were they really after? We never found out that day, but I could have easily found myself in a situation choosing between my values and a few days' sales.

Not all changes were for the worse though. Sometimes in the life of a business, you can get unexpected good surprises, and we were about to get a big one.

RAM'S TIPS:

- Be available for your staff. Keeping an open-door policy helps you get information faster about what is going in the business.

- You can't control what the government or external stakeholders will do next, but you can prepare yourself.

CHAPTER 15

NAIROBI THE BEAUTIFUL

—

In the life of a CEO, there is an inherent conflict between growth, profit, and control. You can only have two of those at a time, and you have to choose carefully. I had chosen profit and control to begin my journey at Green Leaf, but after all the changes we made, we had built scale into the business model. We were ready to switch gears and focus on growth.

A few months after Neha and I celebrated our one-year anniversary since moving to Dar es Salaam, Nijhad called to relate an interesting phone call he had from a contact in Nairobi, Kenya.

Centre Square, a mall ideally located in the city and built over twenty years ago, was erecting a new wing. A local supermarket chain was supposed to anchor that extension, but they had just pulled out and now the landlord was looking for someone to fill the space. Because of its size, none of the other major Kenyan retailers were interested. For us, it was perfect.

If ever there was a space in Nairobi we would have gone into without thinking, it would have been at this mall. It fit exactly the type of clientele we served at Green Leaf, we would get the footfall to build visibility for our brand, and could use this opportunity as a stepping stone to start our regional expansion.

We got in touch with the landlord and arranged a visit. Bijan, the landlord, was traveling shortly so we had to set the meeting for a Sunday afternoon. It worked out perfectly; we could arrive on the Monday prior and do some research before the meeting.

* * *

Despite being a short flight away, Dar and Nairobi couldn't be more different. Dar is set on the Indian ocean; you felt time slow down along with the rolling waves crashing into the beach. The air is hot and humid.

Nairobi is set at almost eighteen hundred meters above sea level, where the air was cool and dry. Its name means "cool water" and is a reference to the river that flows through the city.

As we drove from the airport to our hotel, we could feel the fast pace and excitement that characterized the city. Everywhere cars zoomed past us and people rushed to catch buses that barely stopped at the station.

Tanzanians are typically shy and won't talk much until you start asking questions. Our Kenyan taxi driver interrogated us for the entire two hours we were together. He wouldn't even wait for us to complete our sentence before he had the next question lined up.

"Where did you guys come from?" he asked.

"Tanzania."

"Oh, that's great, I've been to Tanzania before; it's such a beautiful country. What brings you guys here?" he continued.

"We're here on a business tr—"

"Business? What kind of business? he interjected.

"Uh, retail."

"Oh, I have a business as well. I drive this taxi, but I also make t-shirts and uniforms on the side. Are you guys looking for good quality uniforms?"

"No, not really, tha—"

"I will give you a good price! Here, feel my shirt. It's the same material; don't you think it's good quality?"

If one word could be used to describe Nairobi, it would be *hustle*. Everyone was trying to move forward and work hard to go up on the economic ladder. Not only was our new friend driving taxis and selling uniforms, but he also took night classes to study for his MBA.

* * *

How do you do market research in a city you don't know?

First, you read the public research available by the World Bank or other large institutions. It's a good start and gives you a sense of the economy as a whole and the opportunities and challenges on a macro level.

Second, you could hire a market research firm and give them a brief of what you were looking for. However, we wanted to get a firsthand feeling for the market, and reading a report from someone else would not give us that.

> **Lesson #1: The best market research is through direct, one-on-one conversations.**

Together, Nijhad and I had a great network there, him from his family and prior work, me from friends of friends in Dar. We put together a few probing questions to understand people's habits, but the idea was to let them speak. What excited people about being in the city? What did they like or dislike? Where and when did they shop? What did they do with their free time?

A lot revolved around traffic. You could have a supermarket or restaurant one kilometer away, but if you were on the wrong side of a traffic jam, it could take you forty-five minutes to get there! Whatever you did, you had to avoid morning and evening traffic. You were guaranteed to lose hours each way, so you scheduled your meetings or work around that. You slept in and worked late or went to the gym early in the morning or late in the evening to avoid being stuck in a jam. Everyone had a different strategy, but it was all everyone kept referencing.

Talking directly to people also gave us firsthand insights into their habits and mindset. Whenever we met someone and told them our plans, they had an opinion on how we could be successful. Getting all this free advice was great!

What stuck though, from the taxi driver and from everyone we met, was that no matter the economic level, people had ambition and were working to fulfill that. It was perpetually either working while studying or studying while working. The vibe was incredible.

Kenyans also love to shop. We must have gone to a dozen malls, and they were all packed with shoppers at all times of day. Clothing, cosmetics, movie halls, furniture, there was activity in all those stores.

The third leg of our approach to doing research was to have lots of coffee. Specifically, we sat down at coffee shops that were directly in front of supermarket tills and looked at what people were buying. We would make notes of products we saw most often in people's trolleys, how full those trolleys were, and estimate the amount people were spending. We also looked at who the customers were: families shopping with their children, men or women with or without children, dressed in casuals or business wear.

These details added up to give us a profile of our potential future customers.

But the grocery stores were our main focus. There were many large stores with more than five thousand square meters of shopping space where you could find food, of course, but also furniture, mattresses, and even bicycles. Those were more akin to hypermarkets.

Our ambition to open an 850 square meter store was puny in comparison, but that was the point. We weren't going after these large stores, we wanted to compete by providing a differentiated experience with a small store, a more personalized service, and products you couldn't find anywhere else.

Our research repeatedly emphasized one thing. Grocery stores in Kenya had gotten so big, they lost their sense of customer service. And the products they sold were all the same, regardless of the shop you went to. There was no novelty or quality; the market had become stale.

This confirmed our hunch that Green Leaf's value proposition would do well if we could replicate what we had in Dar.

* * *

Finally, Sunday came, and we met with Bijan. Nijhad and I dressed in suits. He was dressed in jeans. We should have done the same.

We spent two hours with him—first in his office where we presented our concept in Dar and plans for the store we would build in Nairobi. Then he took us around the mall and spoke about the concept for the extension they were building.

We visited the space that would eventually become home to the first Green Leaf store outside Tanzania, and we felt a mix of emotions. On the one hand, it was bright and airy with tall ceilings, which gave the sense of a food hall. This would work well with the quality of products we were bringing in. On the other hand, the space seemed to be quite far back, and we were worried about visibility.

Nevertheless, this first meeting was about getting to know each other, and that part was done. We were building a good rapport and liked what the other brought to the table.

Now, Bijan wanted to see one of our stores in action. We set up a day for him to come visit us in Dar about three weeks later when he would be back from his trip overseas. The visit was social but meant to be a negotiation session as well. After he toured our store and we tried to soften him up with butter croissants and fresh coffee, we got down to business.

We sat in that same conference room where we held all our executive meetings; this time there were enough chairs for the three of us.

Bijan's opening bid was high. Then again, who would ever open a bid with a reasonable figure! Besides price, we also needed to negotiate a variety of terms as important as the rental. Those included when we would get the space, how many free months we would have to fit it out, the marketing support from the center, and by how much the rent would grow over time.

Nijhad and I were getting more and more excited about the prospect of opening in Nairobi. Sure, it wouldn't be easy, but one thing I learned from my real estate days is that location was everything. And this was the perfect location for us.

However, another lesson I kept in mind after my experience in Houston was not to let emotions dictate the price. Bijan left that same evening, still with an overall positive feeling, but not a done deal yet. We had to decide if we were fully interested and how much we were willing to pay for that space.

We loved the mall's location, and Bijan's plan for that wing resonated with the Green Leaf concept. However, customers might not easily find us inside the mall since the space was deep inside, and that would mean having to spend more on marketing and potentially taking losses for the first year until we built a steady clientele.

We slept on it and the next day reconvened in the office. Nijhad had come up with an alternative proposal. Instead of paying a fixed rental, we could pay a percentage of our sales. We knew our concept would work in Nairobi, but we were worried about how long it would take for us to get our name out there. That ramp-up phase was critical, and we needed to spend money on building our brand and getting people to know us, not just paying rent.

The way we thought about this, if the store was doing well, then the landlord would do well. If the store was not doing as well, we would have the opportunity to spend more on marketing as we were not tied to a large fixed rental.

The second component was that to promote Green Leaf, there would have to be more signage and more communication from the mall itself to their customers about us. Centre Square had a loyalty program with hundreds of people on their mailing list and having access to those was important. It would be a natural way to start building our customer base.

This was brilliant. We just needed to convince Bijan.

We got on the phone with him that afternoon and relayed our offer.

"Rent is our most important cost, but we need to also focus resources on marketing to ensure people come to our store, and thus come to the mall. So instead of paying a fixed rent, we propose that we pay a percentage of sales. We think 3 percent is fair."

"Hmm I don't usually like percentage of sales because a) I can never be sure how much effort you're putting in, and b) the bank will not give me financing on variable rent. I really prefer fixed rent."

"Ok, you've met us and seen what we've done in Dar. What else could we do to show you we're going to make all the effort required to ensure this store is a success?"

"I have to be sure you guys are committed and that the money you're saving on rent is not just to pay yourselves."

"How about we commit a certain percentage of sales to marketing spent each month? So you can check that for the first year, we will spend, let's say 1 percent of sales on advertising and promotion. Would that work?"

"Yes, that actually would work well. We can put that in the agreement. Now, I also think a long-term lease with variable rent is not fair to me. At some point, you need to be able to pay a fixed rent, no matter your sales level. We can agree to a rent equivalent to 3 percent of sales the first three years, but after that, we revert to the rental amount I had proposed."

It seemed fair. If we still couldn't make it after three years, we would have other problems!

Finally, Bijan also wanted to know if we could open a store in the next six months, that's the timeline he was working on to open the extension. We wanted to be completely transparent: six months was aggressive in our estimate, but we thought we could do it in eight to ten months.

> **Lesson #2: In negotiations, it helps to be objective, transparent, and creative to close a deal.**

We didn't want to oversell on something then under-deliver. He appreciated the honesty and would make it work. Deal done; we were going to open in Nairobi! Now the hard part began.

* * *

We had to assemble a Green Leaf team and supply chain in a new country. Sometimes you don't even know what you don't know. If someone had told me all the challenges we would have to go through to open that store, I'm not sure that in retrospect, I would have gone through with it.

First was the issue of financing. We needed to get a loan from the bank to open an account and borrow funds to buy the equipment for the supermarket. The bank we used in Dar, Ruby Bank, was headquartered in Kenya. Green Leaf had been a customer for over ten years, had borrowed from them multiple times, and repaid those loans without any issues. We thought they would be perfectly willing to lend us money for our planned expansion. We were perfectly wrong!

Although the bank name was the same, the process was completely different and separate. For them, we would be a new client in Kenya, without any history or collateral. Getting a loan would be extremely difficult and time-consuming. We didn't have much time to honor our commitment to Bijan though.

While simultaneously placing orders for the equipment from suppliers in Italy and China, we had to figure out the funds. We put together business plan after business plan, but the managers at Ruby were decidedly not interested.

Things were getting dire. Suppliers had started making equipment on our word, but without payment, they were going to stop soon.

We had initially met a branch manager at Ruby in Nairobi without a formal introduction from Dar. It seemed it would be enough considering our long-standing relationship, but obviously, that was not the case. Ruby had prior bad experiences lending money to supermarkets and was reticent about even looking at our file.

Another lesson from Houston: it was not so much the business plan that mattered in the end, but our passion and motivation for making it work.

That's what we needed to convey to the Ruby team and to the right people who would be willing to take a chance on us. We needed to get to the decision-makers at Ruby Bank in Nairobi and make a more convincing case.

Through our relationship manager in Dar, Nijhad met Ruby Bank's Tanzania CEO and explained what we were planning. Being one of our customers himself who traveled to Nairobi often, he was excited. He immediately put us in touch with Richard, the Head of Corporate Banking in Nairobi.

The next week when Nijhad and I went to Nairobi, we met with Richard. His office was in a tall glass tower owned by the bank, on the sixth floor of a seven-story building.

Richard was a tall, muscular man with a wide smile on his face and a raucous laugh that came out often.

We met him and his analyst and told them how we had gotten nowhere with the branch team and the urgency in getting this loan to set up our store. We showed him all our accounts from Dar, explained the research we had done, how our concept worked, and why we believed it would work in Nairobi.

We told him about Bijan and how impressed he was about our store, the fit with the location, and the extension happening in Central Square.

He went through the business plan, but similar to my meeting with HUB in Houston, he asked about our background and personality. Then he asked more about the research we had done to prove this plan would work. He cared less about the words on the document and more about how much we knew and believed in it. It must have been a bit creepy to hear that we sat in coffee shops for hours on end observing (ok spying) on customers' shopping habits, but it showed our dedication.

We didn't just hire someone else to do the research, but we did it ourselves.

Once again, the numbers and the beautiful presentation we put together didn't matter as much as our conviction.

Lesson #3: The story is as important as your numbers.

We were selling ourselves, and Richard saw how much work we had put into running the stores in Dar. He understood why customers were coming to us. We knew what our competitive advantage was, we had a vision, a mission statement, knew what we did right, how we competed, and where we could make a difference.

After an hour-long meeting, it was sealed. He agreed to review our file and put it forth to the credit committee with a recommendation to go forward on providing the loan. We got the final approval a week later.

We did it! It took many twists and turns, but it all came together just in time. We had the space, and we had the funds. Our Nairobi adventure could now begin.

RAM'S TIPS:

- Market research:

    - Read any public information you can find.

    - Subscribe to online local newspapers of the city in question.

    - Meet as many people as you can and let them talk.

    - Firsthand observation is key.

- Negotiations:

    - Be objective about pros and cons.

    - Be transparent about what you can and cannot do.

    - Be creative. Understand what the other side wants and see if you can reconcile with what you need.

    - Don't let emotions dictate the price.

- Getting a loan:

    - Let your passion and emotion show.

    - Numbers need to be explained with a story.

    - Show the work you've done to get there.

CHAPTER 16

NAIROBI – THE GOOD, THE BAD, AND THE UGLY

Now onto the fun part, designing the store. The overall area was just over 850 square meters, which was a tad smaller than our largest Dar store on the Peninsula.

I had been thinking a lot about modernizing the customer flow inside the supermarket and make it match our concept. This was our chance to get it right, and I spent the next few weeks endlessly Googling photos of Whole Foods, Trader Joe's, Wegman's, and food halls in Europe and South Africa to find inspiration for what the store should look like.

> **Lesson #1: Don't be afraid to challenge the status quo.** Just because you've been doing something a certain way all this time does not mean it can't be improved on.

I also knew from our sales data what customers preferred and could combine this knowledge with supermarket best practices to make a uniquely tailored grocery store for Kenyans. The result was simple, but stark. We left the walls painted white but added lots of lighting all around the store. Above the bakery and the fruits and vegetables sections, we used yellow lighting to emphasize a sense of coziness and warmth. Everywhere else the lights were white to make reading labels easier.

Swahili women wear rectangular cotton cloths called *kanga* in their daily wear. This handmade piece of clothing is very versatile. It can be used as a long dress or skirt, as a head covering for Muslim women, and even as a sling to carry your baby! With its bright colors and patterns, kanga has a historic significance in both Tanzania and Kenya, and each piece includes a Swahili proverb. These proverbs often express hopeful sentiments or good wishes such as "Everything will be fine if you love each other" or "Parents are gold so always take care of them."

A single piece of fabric could have bright red, yellow, orange, blue, or green colors arranged in a certain pattern.

In that same way, I wanted people entering the store to be hit by a multitude of colors arranged in a neat pattern. We decided that the main entrance of the store would be arranged with flowers on the right, the bakery on the left, and the fruits and vegetable section dead center. Flowers would bring the visual mix of colors to your eyes, the bakery with its fresh-smelling bread and pastries would entice your nose, and the produce section—with its green leaves, red tomatoes, yellow bananas, and oranges—would bring order to it all while combining colors and freshness.

Lesson #2: You can find aesthetic inspiration in the every day.

Behind the produce, we would continue with the fresh selection. In a European food hall-style, we set up a cheese and deli counter in a circular fashion at the center of the store. The attendants would stand inside the circle attending to customers looking to buy olives, cheeses, or meats in the open rather than the traditional pre-packaged ones found in other supermarkets.

Next to it was the butchery with more counter space to process fresh meats just like customers wanted. Whether it was prime cuts of beef, spiced sausages, lean minces, burger patties, or marinated chicken, we stood ready with it all.

With fresh shopping done, it was time to get down to the grocery basics with aisles neatly laid out for cereals, pasta, rice, drinks, and, at the back toiletries, home cleaning, pet food, and a small homeware section. The neat thing is that essentials were easy to find. We subscribed to the philosophy that a store should have all its essentials handy so the customer can tick their checklist early and quickly, rather than navigate to the back of the store to find milk and eggs. That always frustrated me, and it was not consistent with our vision.

However, you did have to go through all those other sections to get to the cashier, so there were plenty of opportunities to be tempted!

One point of emphasis was our liquor selection. I spent a considerable amount of time curating beer, wines, and spirits so we had representation from all over the world, small and big supplier alike. We needed to have the cheap 250 milliliters whiskey bottle selling for $1.50, to the premium 750 milliliters Scottish whiskey bottle sitting behind the counter and selling for more than $1,700.

This was part of our philosophy: we didn't judge who you were or what you could afford. Day to day, you might enjoy the regular drink, but for special occasions, you knew you could find exquisite bottles at our store. Or those fancy bottles could serve as an aspiration for you to achieve more and buy them someday. Whatever your personal preferences, we wanted your business. And we took particular care in finding the small local craft brewers to display their product. I saw this across America and Europe, and here, too, people were getting fed up with drinking industrial beer and looking for novelty.

Those suppliers were often too small to be stocked in other stores, but we were just right for them, both in terms of size and customer care.

> **Lesson #3: Remember your vision and mission statement when you're starting something new. Make decisions grounded in them.**

Last, but not least, we needed a team. I started at the top and got lucky. One of our branch managers in Dar, Jeremy, is Kenyan and was keen to come home. He was a natural fit for heading this new branch. He knew all our systems and procedures, but most importantly, he knew Green Leaf and could be the main and most important carrier of our culture from Dar to Nairobi.

> **Lesson #4: Find the culture carriers who can blend the old with the new.**

To help set up the IT and Accounts, we brought Kondo and Balendra over temporarily. Kondo was in charge of recreating our system for Nairobi by hiring an assistant IT analyst and using local consultants to copy and paste our Dar setup. To avoid recruiting a full new accounting team, which would negate the benefits of scale, Balendra hired an accounting firm to maintain our Kenyan books and ensure we were regular with all our taxes. He spent time with them to understand the local intricacies and ensured the team in Dar also picked it up so we could centralize the accounting function there with support from the Kenyan firm. Arnold came back to help with the butchery.

We also hired a Human Resource consultant to help with the paperwork. Although many of the laws between Kenya and Tanzania were similar, it was important to get a local firm to help us navigate the subtleties of Kenyan labor laws and ensure our contracts were fair and equitable to both Green Leaf and the employee. This company would also help us hire staff. We needed forty-five new employees, which, conservatively, meant interviewing nearly 150 people.

Jeremy and I did every single one of those interviews. It was long and gruesome, but I felt it important to hire the first batch of staff to ensure they had the right culture and mindset coming in. The most important criteria I had when selecting candidates was that they should not come from a supermarket background. It sounds counterintuitive, but people who already worked in the industry were set in their ways. Our positioning was unique. The way we treated, almost revered, customers was not comparable to the standard, so whoever we hired had to either come blank or with a fresh mindset.

We went instead with candidates who worked in restaurants and coffee shops. Teaching them how to merchandise a shelf would be the easy part. Most people hired were young, many younger than twenty-five, but they were keen and eager to work with us.

We gave them three full days of training with case studies and role-plays on most scenarios they would encounter when dealing with customers. I led the training sessions and began role-plays by pretending I was a customer.

"Excuse me, I need some pasta. Where is your pasta section?"

"Over there, sir."

First strike, you never ever point a customer to where they should go. You take them there yourself.

"Do you have tomato sauce?"

"Yes, sir, we have these three kinds of sauces."

"What about tomato sauce with mushroom and garlic? Do you have that one?"

"It's not here on the shelf, sir."

Second strike, you're not supposed to be looking with the customer. You should always know what is on your shelf or what is in stock; you are its owner.

"Do you also have fresh breads?"

"Yes, sir, let me take you to our bakery section."

"Does this have a lot of salt? I can't eat much salt."

"I don't know, sir."

Third strike, if you don't know, you immediately find someone who does. Don't leave the customer hanging.

It was intense, but they were getting it. At the end, I felt good about the incoming team's enthusiasm.

> **Lesson #5: Be an integral part of the hiring and training, especially with the first batch of employees.**

We had figured the logistics for most sections but hit a roadblock with two of the most critical ones: the bakery and the fresh produce.

Our bakery team in Dar was at full capacity, and we couldn't get anyone to come and help us. Getting this right was important. I knew from Dar that many of our customers came to get bread first thing in the morning, and then did the rest of their shopping.

As for fresh produce, we wanted the best quality but also knew the high cost of running such a section. Fruits perish daily, and in the early days, while we were still building a following, we wanted to be able to control our losses.

In both cases, the answer came in the form of a partnership. For the bakery, we teamed up with a local outfit called Bread Box. Nijhad met the owner, Dean, through friends of friends, and we immediately loved their breads. In many ways, it reminded us of what we made in Dar, and so we offered him a partnership for the bakery section.

We would buy the equipment and set up according to his standards. In exchange, he would provide the production team, recipes, and the sales team. We would co-brand as Bread Box by Green Leaf, which would help us associate with a well-known bakery in Nairobi. For Dean, this would be the second location he was dreaming about.

Mistake #1: Don't confuse dream with execution capabilities.

As we were feverishly setting up the equipment, a woman walked into the site one day. We had many people peeking to see what was happening inside, so were used to telling them to please stay away as this was still a construction site, but soon it would be a one-of-a-kind grocery store.

Malia, after barging through the safety curtains, started peppering me with questions even before I could lead her out.

I was getting annoyed, as we had a lot of work to finish that day. I didn't want to upset a potential future customer, so I went along as politely as I could.

Suddenly, she pulled out a business card. She owned a fruits and vegetable distribution business and wanted to discuss if she could supply to us.

Maybe this was the break I was looking for!

We went and sat down for tea and started discussing how we could work together. Malia supplied a few smaller supermarkets throughout the city but was looking to aggressively grow her business. She seemed like a sharp businesswoman and had a good pulse on what customers were looking for.

"I would like to supply you with our fruits and vegetables. We have the best quality available in the city, and I can guarantee you customers will come to Green Leaf only for those."

"That is a strong statement. Good produce will definitely give our customers a sense of the high quality we are pushing toward, but if the quality is bad, then it will also ruin the entire store experience."

"Yes, but it won't be. I can promise you that."

"Ok, if you can promise that, why don't we set up a partnership instead of a straight supplier agreement."

"What do you mean?"

"You will be our exclusive supplier of fruits and vegetables and get to control the entire section. You choose what will be stocked, the quantity, price, display, etc., with our input of course. In exchange, we will take 20 percent of the sales and you keep the rest."

"That sounds interesting, so I get to keep any profits above the 20 percent of sales? And what happens to any damages?"

"That's also on you. If you know that our customers will love what you sell, then there shouldn't be many losses and a big profit for you."

"Ok, I haven't done this type of arrangement before, so let's do it, but I think 15 percent commission to you would be fairer."

I knew from Dar that we expected to make 20 percent in this section, but we controlled it ourselves and had the headache of dealing with orders and damaged produce. I didn't have the luxury of time to negotiate, and our opening was now a month away. Outsourcing this section felt like a good way to tackle it, so we agreed.

> **Mistake #2: Make sure you understand your partner's business model to ensure alignment.**

Our set up was good. Getting to where we were had been a challenge, but I was getting high on success and feeling unstoppable. This would be one of many stores in Nairobi.

> **Mistake #3: Feelings of success breed complacency, which, in turn, leads to oversight.**

Finally, we needed a marketing strategy. We decided to first only focus on the Central Square customers by blasting their email list with our opening date and location within the mall. However, because of the short timelines we had been pushing, we decided to keep the information to a minimum. We didn't have any specific products to advertise or opening specials.

At that time, it seemed like a good idea to start with just telling people we existed and not explaining what made us different.

> **Mistake #4: Rushing causes mistakes. Marketing is critical, so take the time to explain to your customers what makes you so special.**

* * *

On Monday, April 23, 2018, at noon, we opened Green Leaf Nairobi. This felt like a vindication of the plan Nijhad and I discussed almost three years ago when we met in that Scandinavian coffee shop in New York.

After all those months of hard work planning, designing the store, hiring staff, and stocking shelves, it felt incredibly good to see customers trickling in. That Monday was a holiday and Central Square was packed; we would get good visibility from people walking in. Free marketing!

Now that the store was open, I was planning to make a big splash in newspapers and billboards all around the mall to announce our arrival. I breathed a sigh of relief. All had gone without a hitch.

Bijan also came by later that afternoon to congratulate us. As we were talking, Jeremy walked over and asked to talk to me.

"Is everything ok, Jeremy?"

"No, sir, I think we have a problem. There seems to be an issue with the tills at check-out."

I looked over and could see a big line of customers queuing with their baskets and trolleys. That would normally be a good sign, except the line was not moving.

"Is the line not moving Jeremy?"

"Whenever we scan certain items, they don't show up on the screen. So an attendant has to run to the shelf, find the price, and we have to manually enter it. It's happening with almost half the products for every customer, so people are getting annoyed and angry."

I rushed over to see the situation for myself, and it didn't look good.

We had been open less than two hours and were now realizing that, somehow, products had not been entered correctly in the system. Many supplier invoices had not been uploaded onto the server. In our rush to open, we spent only a few hours doing testing instead of multiple days. We randomly picked the few products that happened to work fine, but many were not.

Some other products had the wrong prices. On the files that were uploaded, the price column had been accidentally moved by one row, so all products now had the wrong price.

What a disaster this was turning out to be. What should have been a crowning achievement was turning into an unmitigated disaster.

And now the free marketing I hoped we would get by opening the day of a big holiday would turn into a nightmare, with more and more customers turned off by our lack of competence.

> **Mistake #5: Don't open right before a big holiday in anticipation of crowds. You need time to figure out how things will go in the beginning.**

We had no choice now. I shut down the store immediately, letting the last few customers slowly process their purchase, then I immediately got to work.

We had already advertised we were open so didn't have the luxury of waiting until the next day to debrief on the situation and figure out the next steps. So, along with Jeremy and Kondo and some of the confused new staff that we asked to stay and help us, we spent all night going through every single aisle, picking every single product, and checking that the item existed in our system and was priced correctly.

It took us almost eighteen hours of non-stop work, but the next day, Tuesday, April 24, 2018, at 1:00 p.m., we finally opened the store without any glitches this time.

The second time around was exhilarating, probably because I had drunk so much coffee and hadn't slept all night, but we had done it. We had expanded to another country. We faced so many challenges in the last few years, months, days, and even hours, but now we were open for good in Kenya.

The next couple of days I caught a bit more sleep but always made sure to be at the store with the first shift opening at 7:00 a.m., and stay until we closed at 9:00 p.m. I sat for hours in a seating area right outside our store, watching customers walking in and out, talking to some of them about their experiences and how we could do better.

I realized our hubris caused us to miss an important step in the opening process and wanted to make sure nothing else dramatic happened. Right on cue, our partnership with Dean and Malia unraveled within the first two weeks of opening.

Dean had operated only out of a single location, and he was not organized enough to operate this second one. The breads came out way too early and didn't look fresh by the time customers bought them. Pastries were late; no one looked to buy pies or rolls in the middle of the afternoon. And the cakes, which looked so beautiful in his store, looked dull and unappealing in ours because he didn't have enough decorating materials.

With Malia, it was a different story. She was indeed shrewd. When she noticed customers were slow to trickle in, she quickly reduced the quantities of fruits and vegetables supplied. With produce, the more you see stacked up, the more you want to buy. And the less you see, the less you feel like buying.

If you see three bananas on a shelf, you're unlikely to pick any of them, thinking they're the last of the batch and of poor quality. If you see dozens and dozens of bunches, you will feel good about the quality.

The vicious cycle quickly dented our sales not only of produce but of the entire store. Customers saw the dull bakery and drab produce section right at the entrance of the store and associated all our products with this poor quality.

For different reasons, but leading to the same outcome, we canceled our agreements with Dean and Malia and decided to do it ourselves. We were fortunate that at the same time in Dar, the low season was starting, so we convinced Marcus, our head baker, to come help us in Nairobi for a few months until we could build out the team.

Jeremy and I started going to the central produce market in downtown Nairobi three times a week, loaded a van full of the best stuff we could find, and brought it back to stock up the shelves before the store opened. Sweat the small stuff, as they say!

Eventually, we met local producers in the market who agreed to supply us directly in the store, and we didn't have to do the rounds ourselves.

* * *

If I was to redo our Nairobi adventure, I would change a few things. Nothing will go as perfectly as you want, but the aim was to launch the store and quickly learn to become the best we could be. We worked hard, we made mistakes, and we learned from them.

We managed to open in a new country in a record time, built a store with products that responded to the market demand, and set up a really strong team. However, in the rush, we didn't test our system fully, got carried away on our own feelings of uniqueness without explaining it to customers, and trusted people without proper accountability.

If we hadn't rushed this way, perhaps we wouldn't have lost some early customers who will only remember the long lines and poor produce selection of the early days.

My impatience pushed us to get there, and the team followed. More than anything I learned about the grocery business those past three years, I felt I had grown as a manager. A business is not just a collection of products on the shelves and a bank account, it's about people. And in the end, opening in Nairobi was the right call.

Thanks to the help and support of the people around Nijhad and I, we accomplished the initial vision for Green Leaf and grew it from a single country supermarket chain to an East African supermarket chain.

RAM'S TIPS:

- When expanding your business:

  - Don't be afraid to rethink certain aspects (like the design or layout). If you can improve on the status quo, do it.

  - Stick with your vision and mission statement. Let them guide what you change and what you keep.

  - Test and retest to make sure you're ready before the big day.

- Don't rush unless you're ready, and don't let feelings of hubris or complacency make you skip critical steps in the process.

- Building a new team:

  - Find a culture carrier who can be a bridge between the old and the new.

  - The first employees are critical. No matter the level, be involved in the interview process. This will set the right tone and help emphasize your culture.

  - When hiring, focus on attitude more than on experience. It's easier to train people in the way you want things done than to change someone's mindset into a hard worker.

  - In the same vein as interviewing, make sure you're part of the training.

- Building partnerships:

  - Understand your partner(s) experiences and motivation. Make sure they are aligned with yours.

PART 3

SELL

"Buy with the exit in mind."

CHAPTER 17

THE RAISE

———

It had now been more than two years since that first trip to Nairobi. We'd had many successes and challenges to overcome, but in mid-2019, it felt like we had finally reached a steady point with the business.

Besides opening in Nairobi, we also opened a store in Arusha. We now had five stores in Tanzania and one in Kenya, and all were doing reasonably well. We had the concept right, set up our systems and processes, invested in training our people, and were ready to scale up even more.

But where we? Or rather, was I ready to scale more?

I was exhausted. I didn't feel any sense of satisfaction from what we had accomplished. Others complimented us on how we had grown, but to me, it was a hollow victory.

Since opening the store in Nairobi, I was spending more and more time there. Every other week, I took an early Monday morning flight and returned way past dinner time on Fridays. Often, I spent the weekend there to ensure everything was running smoothly during our busy days.

In Dar, things weren't calm either. All the work I did not attend to during my trips to Kenya sat there waiting for when I got back. I often spent late nights and weekends in the office going through paperwork.

This was starting to have a toll on my relationship with Neha. Even when I was around, I was too exhausted to do anything or too short-tempered to have a simple conversation.

Lesson #1: Growth is exciting and inspiring, but also draining.

In Nairobi, I was "the boss," which meant that even if I was friendly with the staff, they were not my friends.

I spent every meal eating alone, almost always at the office. Jeremy would invite me to dinner at his house, but I never went. Early at Green Leaf, I had realized that I could not engage socially with anyone at the office the same way I used to when I had peers.

Politics in an office is a real issue, no matter the culture you try and create. If anyone felt I was favoring another employee, by, say, going to their home for dinner, then how could they trust I was objective? I had to make decisions that were not always popular, but the employees needed to know I was doing it for the greater good of Green Leaf, free from any bias.

If you read books on entrepreneurship, you'd find that to counter loneliness, you need to enhance your well-being and prioritize your family and friends. Taking time off, going on vacation, and setting boundaries at work are all important for your mental health and, ultimately, benefit the business thanks to your clearer thinking.

I was far from doing that and had no way of closing the gap.

Lesson #2: Entrepreneurship is an incredibly lonely journey.

Besides the loneliness and lack of balance, there was also a gap between the perceived success of the business and the personal financial achievements.

The money for growth didn't only come from the banks but also personal sacrifices. Nijhad and I took a small salary. Every week I flew in economy. People we met seemed to think that because I owned the business, I got groceries for free or at cost. We weren't concerned about the money we spent on groceries but the unnecessary insinuations when all your sweat and mind space is spent running the business. Neha and I made a point from the beginning to always pay for everything we bought to ensure every employee shifted their mindset from "this is a family business" to "we work for a professional company."

The value of the business was growing, but it didn't mean I was taking in cash. On the contrary, investing for growth meant constantly deciding to forgo today's pleasure for hopefully more in the future.

Because we were reinvesting all excess cash flow to fund growth and expansion, many times, I looked at our bank statement and we had just enough to make the payroll and buy some inventory to carry over the next month's activities. How is one supposed to be excited and motivated when constantly facing this situation?

> **Lesson #3: Even if the business is doing well, you may not be personally earning more.**

* * *

Things came to a breaking point after a particularly exhausting trip to Nairobi. As I landed back in Dar, I felt a sharp pain below my neck. At first, I thought I must have not slept well the night before or hunched over my laptop too much.

The pain wouldn't go away even after a few days, and when I couldn't turn my head anymore without huffing, Neha took me to a doctor. The x-ray was clear: my muscles were so tense that, when they pushed one of my bones, it directly compressed my spinal cord.

The doctor said he hadn't seen this in anyone below the age of forty-five. Here I was in my mid-thirties, suffering like someone ten years older.

This couldn't go on anymore.

On the way back from the doctor's, Neha and I started discussing what to do next.

Worried, she wanted me to stop traveling for the next month, even stay away from the office for a few weeks. In the heat of the moment, she didn't even want me on my phone or laptop!

"You're right, honey, I have been thinking the same thing."

Since I couldn't keep my hands off the phone and was on call even on weekends and during vacations, Neha probably expected me to put up more of a fight. I didn't because I was also processing the doctor's words and my own weariness from the past months.

As we talked, we went from the initial emotional kneejerk reaction to talking more deliberately about what we wanted.

"Neha, I've been thinking more and more about how much we want to commit to this business. Personally, I mean. We're still far from our initial plan, but I don't know if I can do it anymore. It's difficult being away from you, and although the business is growing, I'm not growing personally."

"Well, what do you want out of this business? Have you looked back at what you and Nijhad had set out to do all those years ago?"

I hadn't thought about it for a long time now. Our initial plan for Green Leaf was three-fold. First, fix and set it up for scale. Second, raise capital to grow. Third, exit.

"So the answer is simple, you need to raise capital," she answered.

"That will mean longer hours, more work."

"I don't think there are many more hours left for you to work, but the truth is, you want to build a big business. That was always the goal. You didn't buy Green Leaf to run a lifestyle business and for us to settle in Dar with just the four stores. That's why we've made the tough decisions and financial choices we did, so you could become the premier East African supermarket. I just don't want you to kill yourself over it."

I was burning out because I over-extended phase one into phase two. I was scaling up the business, but still with limited resources. To achieve our vision, it was time to move on to phase two.

We needed capital not only to open new stores but also to hire a bigger management team who could take the pressure off me.

To help us do this, we engaged a financial advisor, Sunrise Capital.

* * *

At our first meeting with Sunrise, we were hopeful. We had built a good story from the day we acquired Green Leaf, to the improvements we made in the company's systems and processes, and finally to proving our expansion in Nairobi was working. At first glance, it all added up and we could be a compelling investment.

Over the next few weeks, Sunrise started the process of putting together an Information Memorandum, a document summarizing to potential investors what our business was all about and how we planned to use their funds to grow.

Putting it together required gathering all sorts of information from us. It started with our historical financials, of course, but also included our strategy, road map for growth, our vision and mission statement, details on our import processes, our information systems, top suppliers, and the management team.

It was burdensome to provide all this but necessary in order to put our best foot forward for potential investors. After two months of back and forth, delving into all aspects of our business, there it was: the information memorandum. Just a few pages summed up years of work!

> **Lesson #4: Financial investors can turbocharge your growth, but they have high expectations on profit and timeline.**

Sunrise aimed to send the memorandum to financial investors targeting East Africa, mainly those running private equity funds. Those types of investors looked to give money to smart entrepreneurs who have an established business and need fresh capital to grow quickly over the following years. A typical investment lasted five to seven years, with the investors expecting to double their capital in that period.

On paper, we met all those criteria. In practice though, our bubble was quickly deflated.

Tanzania was no longer the attractive investment destination it used be. The current government had been elected on an anti-corruption platform and positive message for companies. However, the atmosphere had quickly turned sour. Business was seen as the problem, and businesspeople were vilified. Taxes and various costs of doing business were increasing day by day.

I had seen this happening firsthand, but like everyone else, initially thought this was temporary, an adjustment for a newly elected government looking to make its mark.

First, they increased the tax rates.

Then, they mandated more costly licenses for operating a business.

Next, they increased duties on importing products even if they could not be found locally.

Finally, they cracked down on immigrant employment eligibility and requirements, making it harder to hire people with the right expertise.

Our customers were also bearing the brunt of these shifts in policies. When major employers faced increasing business costs, they laid off people. Others were feeling the pinch of increased taxes and had to cut back their spending. Getting a work visa was getting harder, and people who had been in the country for years were not getting theirs renewed and had to leave in a hurry. Many of them owned businesses and had to simply shut down and leave.

Our customer base was suffering for all these reasons. Slowly, but surely, sales started to slow down. I was part of multiple business groups, and all of us hoped this was temporary.

For financial investors who have a limited time span to invest in a business, it did not look good. With a five-year horizon, losing one year to a recession means you've lost 20 percent of the time needed to make your profit.

Why take that risk when there was a compelling opportunity in another country nearby and they could always take a wait-and-see approach? If things did improve, they could choose to invest then.

We had started to diversify when we opened in Nairobi, but sadly, on January 15, 2019, gunmen affiliated with the terrorist group Al-Shabaab attacked a hotel and office complex in the heart of the city, less than ten kilometers from our store, where I was at that time. The Kenyan security services quickly managed to gain control of the situation, but not before the terrorists killed more than twenty people.

As soon as the attack happened, the mall sent out an alert for all shops to close. We urgently shut down the store and organized taxis to send our staff home. Security was the priority, and I ensured everyone had left before leaving the store myself.

The next day, the mood was somber. Everyone was scared. I was scared. I was alone in Nairobi. Neha was alone in Dar. Now it was usually only a few days at a time, not the weeks on end that were required when I first opened the store here, but something like this makes you think, *Is it worth traveling so much and being far from your loved one?*

* * *

Following the terrorist attack in Nairobi, our business decreased sharply. Customers didn't want to come into malls where they could be trapped if something happened. And when they came, they focused on their shopping list and quickly left, not taking the time anymore to look at the new products we had gotten or taste the latest flavors from the bakery.

We lost 40 percent of our business overnight, and even months later, we were still 25 percent off the pre-terrorist attack level.

But I was not about to give up just yet.

Steven Schwarzman, the head of Blackstone, one of the largest private equity funds in the world, still talks about the hundreds of meetings he did and the number of rejections he got when trying to raise their first fund. He remembers being stood up by the MIT endowment fund on a late summer Friday, then trying to hail a cab in the rain to get back to the airport and him and his partner being drenched. After just coming out of running the Mergers & Acquisitions group at one of the most prestigious Wall Street firms, that would have been quite a humbling experience.[15] If he didn't stop after so many rejections, why should I? Time to put my thinking hat on.

RAM'S TIPS:

- Combat loneliness in your work. You can't single-handedly change your company, grow it, and lead a team effectively.

- Beware the financial and health stress of managing and growing a business. There is a personal cost in achieving success.

- Lifestyle Business vs. Building an Empire. You can choose to run a business as is without taking outside investment or reinvesting. If you want to build a larger company, you will need to constantly reinvest or even raise outside capital to grow locations and stores.

- Financial investors can turbocharge your growth, but they are short term by nature. Keep in mind their investment horizon when looking to raise funds from them, and make sure it is appropriate for your business and vision.

---

15 Stephen A. Schwarzman, *What It Takes: Lessons in the Pursuit of Excellence* (New York: Simon & Schuster, 2019), 1-2.

CHAPTER 18

FOOD FOR THOUGHT

We were struggling to think about the future. What could we do if we just had these six stores running in two countries? Without capital to grow, we were neither here nor there.

The plan was for an expansion throughout the region, and I had invested a lot to get to this point. Time, sweat, energy, money. Many sleepless nights went into Green Leaf, and without further capital and a bigger team, I was not sure how we could do more.

The business in Dar was facing challenges, but the team was well-trained and focused. They could resolve most problems they faced on their own. It was gratifying to see this group of people that had a hard time talking to each other just a few years ago working together so well to adjust to the situation.

I wasn't needed much anymore for the day-to-day operations in Dar but was instrumental in figuring out how to scale up the machine we had created. If we couldn't grow, I wasn't sure the team would remain excited for very long. To be honest, I wasn't quite sure I would be excited running the business either. I was looking to build something larger. A lifestyle business was not what Nijhad or I had set up to do.

Likewise, I wasn't particularly excited about simply waiting for the macroeconomic environment to improve and for private equity investors to start investing again. We could have raised money from family and friends. After all, I had done it during my Texas days, but we didn't want that kind of capital. The funds would be too small to plan the big expansion we sought, and it still wouldn't help us hire more senior talent.

I had lunch with Neha, and we seriously discussed our future. We had moved here almost four years ago, and she was an integral part of every major decision. She had also seen the toll it takes to build a store one by one with limited capital and resources; it was not fun.

No, we just couldn't do what we had done so far. We needed to think and execute big. Nairobi was a bigger market with plenty of opportunities. I got on the phone with Nijhad.

"Ram, what's on your mind?"

"We need to raise funds somehow. Even if it's going to take us hundreds of calls all over the globe, we will get it done."

"There has to be a better way. People outside Tanzania are seeing the problems and it's scaring them away. I think we should focus on finding investors within the country. What do you think?"

"You know the current situation as well as I do. Who here would be investing right now?"

"Everyone who is already invested and wants to expand," he replied. "When the economy is difficult, that's when businesspeople spot an opportunity and invest. They have been here for generations and witnessed much more difficult times than what we're seeing now. Their time frame is not five years like the private equity funds; their time frames are generational."

Nijhad was right. I had come from a private equity background so always looked at it from that lens, but the local business community had the money and the conviction. They had been here for decades and seen the ups and downs. Besides, many of them shopped at Green Leaf and loved the store. Perhaps we could convince one of them to invest.

Lesson #1: When looking for investors, make a list of everyone you know who would be a good fit with your business, the company culture, and understand what they could gain by investing.

I started by making a list of every businessperson I knew in Tanzania. I removed from my list those I knew were going through a really difficult time, and those with similar businesses to Green Leaf and who might, under the pretense of investing, try to get information only to leave us hanging at the last minute.

The list was short—just three names. Three chances to keep the dream alive.

* * *

Just as I was about to approach the first contact, Amir, the former owner, was coming back from one of his regular trips to London. He had multiple businesses in Dar to attend to and was combining this one with attending the upcoming Green Leaf board meeting.

Nijhad and I gave him the update. As he heard about the plan to reach out to local businesspeople, his eyes widened. I was fully prepared to hear a lecture on how we should be careful who we speak to and if word got out of the raise, people wouldn't think we were growing but actually doing poorly. That was typical of a small business community, always worried about what the next person is thinking.

"Why are you reaching out to these three people?"

"Because they have the financial capability to invest and would likely be interested in Green Leaf. I know them quite well, and they are trustworthy."

"Yes, I know they are, but I have a better idea. Why don't I buy you out instead?"

I almost fell off my chair. Had I heard this right?

"What do you mean buy us out?"

"I mean I will buy back your stake in Green Leaf. That business has always been in my heart, and I know the challenges today are temporary. It might take two years or ten years, but the business will come back and grow like it always has in this country."

Amir was also tired of retirement and was keen on jumping back into the action. He knew the business inside out and realized how much we had transformed it for the better in the last few years. And he loved to control his own destiny. This was an opportunity for him to take back his business, but without the issues that used to haunt him.

We had spent time streamlining the operations, revamping the systems and processes, and establishing clear roles and responsibilities for all staff. He didn't have to micro-manage every aspect anymore, could know exactly how the business was doing at all times, and knew that the team was working harmoniously. This meant he could focus on just what he enjoyed: the customer experience and finding new products to stock.

Most importantly, he was willing to be patient and wait for the economic situation to improve. Once it did, he could continue investing in Tanzania and Kenya.

Nijhad and I were between two minds about this unexpected offer.

This was most definitely not the plan. We had realized phase one and now were excited about moving on to phase two. Selling now would mean leaving value on the table, but then again, we couldn't afford to be as patient as Amir. If it did take ten years for the economy to recover, were we willing to wait out that long?

"Nijhad, what do you think?"

"I'm not sure what to think. It's not what we set out to do, but... can we even still achieve the rest of our plan?"

"Yes, I agree this was not part of the plan, but then again, only fools don't change their minds! On a serious note though, it's not phase two of our plan, but we're directly going to phase three, the exit. We should consider it in that lens instead."

"I see what you mean. And in that lens, are you ready to sell?"

Was I ready? This was the question I asked myself even before buying Green Leaf, how would I know I was ready?

Deep inside, I knew the answer.

"I feel ready. We came on this journey almost four years ago and set ourselves ambitious goals. We've achieved most of them in an incredibly short period of time. We could do more, but the macro-economic situation is against us. Although I enjoyed our time in Dar and Nairobi, I can't see myself here for the next ten years waiting for things to change. We're not the right people to write the next chapter of the Green Leaf story."

Not only that, but I also felt like I had achieved my Plan, the one I had rehearsed at the five-year reunion. I wanted to become a better investor by running a company, going deep into operations, and develop my business intuition. These last few years I had done exactly that.

Nijhad agreed. He also knew this was the best way forward.

We set ourselves a selling price based on what we thought valued where the business had come to and the future potential we had positioned it for. Since taking over, we'd grown sales by over 50 percent with the new store openings and almost doubled cash flow thanks to all the initiatives on reducing costs and stock-outs.

If this worked, the implications were huge. After creating our lives in Dar, Neha and I would have to find a new home. What would we do? Where would we go? It was unclear then, but one thing was certain, we would figure it out together.

After some back and forth with Amir, we sold the business the same way we had acquired it: by looking at a multiple of cash flow. The business had grown since we took over, we negotiated the multiple and finally agreed to a deal.

On a handshake, it was done. We were leaving Tanzania.

RAM'S TIPS:

- Raising money from family and friends is tedious and emotionally challenging. You can do it in the early stages, but when you need to grow fast, this is not the best avenue.

- Financial investors can provide you a large amount of capital to grow quickly and hire more people. However, they are often constrained by short-term horizons. In many regions and sectors, this model has proven inappropriate.

- Family investors or corporations, on the other hand, can take a longer-term view or generational approach. They are willing to invest when conditions are difficult and wait for things to improve to reap the rewards.

- Finding an investor is like finding the right partner: understand if there is a fit with your business and culture.

CHAPTER 19

SAYING OUR FAREWELL

The end was bittersweet. We didn't leave Green Leaf exactly how we had planned. It would have been much bigger and different if we could have realized our full vision. However, we did leave it in a better place than we had found it.

What now?

Fortunately, we had time to plan for our future. Drawing up the documents took a few weeks, and we prepared a three-month transition plan split between Dar and Nairobi to ensure everything was handed over properly.

I needed to inform the key staff personally for three reasons.

First, I wanted to make sure this was taken as a positive sign for the company. Someone would be willing to invest in taking Green Leaf to the next level, so no one had to worry about their future.

Second, I could explain my rationale. I didn't expect everyone to agree with the decision, but I felt like I owed them an explanation for why we weren't continuing on the same path.

Third, we had been through so much together and I wanted to express how grateful I was for the journey. I wanted to explain how much I appreciated their hard work and learned from them over the past years.

Over the course of two days, I scheduled individual lunches and coffee with Balendra, Neema, Kabir, Sandra, Kondo, Samir, and the rest of the senior team. I opened the same way, by explaining where we had come from and how far we had come to get to where we were. I told them how proud I was of what he had built together, but now it was time for me to move on. The next chapter of Green Leaf would be great, but it would be without me.

> **Lesson #1: Even when leaving, communicate in an honest and transparent way with your staff.**

* * *

The most emotional conversation was with Balendra. I absorbed a lot from other people in the company, but in this department, since I had some prior experience, we spent a lot of time learning from each other.

We chose one of our favorite Indian restaurants. He introduced me to it when we first arrived in Dar, and Neha and I ate there at least twice a month. Oddly enough, it was a racquet club where you had to spend $1 per person as a cover charge just to enter.

The restaurant was essentially a large open-air area with cement floors, uncoordinated plastic chairs and tables with various shades of sun-burnt reds and blues, and a projector on one end showing eighties Bollywood music videos. The weirdness of the atmosphere was only rivaled by the quality of the food, which was phenomenal.

It was one of those rare places where the chef didn't change the recipes to accommodate local tastes but, instead, chose to create authentic Indian dishes as they are made in India. He stayed true to himself, which was fitting to what I was about to share with Balendra about my next move.

I had rehearsed my words a few times with Neha and managed to control the flow of tears in my eyes. It was harder for Balendra to control his emotions.

"But Ram, why are you leaving? We are finally putting things under control. How are we going to manage without you?"

"The same way you've been doing it all this time. Trust your instincts, discuss things with everyone, and you'll come to the right decision."

"Have you gotten a job somewhere else? That is not right to leave us for another job like this; you are abandoning us!"

"No, Balendra, I don't have another job. I am sorry you feel I am abandoning you, but that is not what I want to do. I was the right person to help manage the business these last few years, but I am not right anymore for the future."

"Please, you must reconsider. Think about all the things we can accomplish!"

"You will still accomplish them! Choosing to sell was one of the hardest decisions I ever made in my life, but I sincerely believe it's for the best of the company. I wish all the success in the world for Green Leaf, but this chapter for me is closing and it's time to look for my next opportunity. I don't know yet what it will be, but I can only hope I will work with a team as talented as each of you were. I learned so much over these last years, not only about the grocery business but also about leadership and myself; I owe this to you."

Disbelief, then anger, and finally sadness came with the acceptance of my departure. It wasn't easy on anyone, but I was determined to make this a positive experience.

That's also when I learned from Neema that when I first joined the company, some of the staff had secretly placed bets I wouldn't last six months! To them, I was a foreigner who had never lived in Tanzania, had no experience in grocery retail or even running a business, and someone they thought had never done anything other than work on a computer in an office. I wouldn't have given myself much chance either.

But it worked, and the journey was fantastic, in no small part thanks to each of them.

The Nairobi store needed a lot more handling, as the team was new and in a different country than headquarters, but Jeremy had been present from the start, and I knew he could lead the team and the transition process.

Although I had been with them the shortest time, the Nairobi staff was the hardest to say goodbye to. I had recruited each one of them, and we had spent time in the trenches— role-playing in interviews, putting products on the shelf together, opening and closing the store together many days, and waiting with bated breath for the computer to tell us our sales for that day.

I announced my departure in a morning staff meeting, and I got so emotional that I had to leave the store early.

Even though it wasn't the case, I felt like I was letting everyone down. We were supposed to be in this journey together. Why was I jumping ship? I knew the reasons and really believed it wouldn't be a good fit to stay, but in those moments when you see everyone else's reaction around you, it makes you wonder.

Could I have raised the money and stayed? Maybe we can stay on and partner with Amir? Is there another way to keep being involved with Green Leaf?

> **Lesson #2: Business is emotional. Don't be afraid to second-guess your decision and check with your gut that "it feels right."**

The decision was made, and it was right. It was already a roller-coaster ride to get to this point and the fundamental reasons for moving had not changed. The economic prospects were still uncertain, which made raising private capital to grow and hire a bigger team impossible. And I had achieved my original Plan.

* * *

After about twelve weeks of working with staff, our key suppliers, bankers, and landlords, I had done the bulk of our transition work but remained available, as loose items always pop up suddenly.

Since we were leaving soon, Neha and I wanted to see and soak up as much of Tanzania as we could. We took a three-day weekend off and planned one last memorable trip.

The plan was to first fly to Mbeya, in the Southwest. We wanted to spend time in the cooler hills exploring farms and coffee plantations, and then head to Lake Nysa near the border with Malawi. Unfortunately, as a reminder that things don't always work out as planned, our ninety-minute flight was first delayed by eight hours, then finally canceled with no alternatives until the next day.

Instead of letting this bring our spirits down, we quickly made new plans and took the two-hour ferry to Zanzibar and stayed in Stone Town for one last exciting trip along the Swahili Coast.

Stone Town is the old part of Zanzibar City and the former capital of the Zanzibar Sultanate. Until the nineteenth century, it was a flourishing center for spice and slave trading.

The streets are too narrow for cars but wide enough for multiple bicycles, motorbikes, and street vendors moving carts of goods around the city. Walking in that part of town always felt magical. You never knew what amazing historical building you would find around the corner, or which beautiful colors the residents had decided to paint their house.

Its unique mix of Swahili and Arab traders, along with Persian, Indian, and European influence, has given the city a very specific architectural style and earned it a designation as a UNESCO World Heritage Site.

Most buildings have two key features. The first is a large veranda protected by carved wooden balustrades.

The second, and best-known aspect of Zanzibari houses, are the large and finely decorated wooden doors and windows. They often have rich carvings and bas-reliefs, and some of them have big brass studs that served as knockers. The shape and size of the door, as well as the intricacy of the carvings, indicated the wealth and origin of the trader.

Arab traders had carvings with Islamic content and rectangular-shaped door openings. Indian traders most often used Hindu symbolism like lotus flowers and rounded door openings.

We stayed in a hotel emblematic of the style, one of our favorites, with each room decorated differently than the others with unique pieces of antiques and ceilings carved out of wood. The most astonishing part of the hotel is its rooftop. It is only nine floors high but stood tall above other buildings in Stone Town and gave spectacular views of the sun setting over the Indian Ocean.

That evening was a particularly extraordinary one. We had seen beautiful sunsets during our time here, but never before had we witnessed such an explosion of reds, pinks, and oranges coloring the sky.

It felt like watching the Northern Lights, but warmer.

Maybe it was destiny that our trip to Mbeya didn't work out and we came here instead—a reminder that even if your original plan doesn't work out the way you want, life has a funny way of making it up to you.

RAM'S TIPS:

- Always plan more time than you think is needed for a transition.

  - Be honest and transparent to your staff about why you're leaving.

  - Keep a positive tone. The best sign of your positive contribution is that the company continues to thrive after you're gone.

  - Strive to leave things better than when you found them.

- It's ok to be emotional in business. If you need to second-guess your decision, do it and make sure it "feels right." This is a critical part of building your intuition!

- If your original plan doesn't work, it's ok! Find an alternative and make the best of it.

CHAPTER 20

WAS IT WORTH IT?

Yes, it was!

Despite all the challenges I went through—doing every job at the company, the first executive meeting, opening up in Nairobi, attempting to raise capital—I would re-do it in a heartbeat. Every single step I took with Green Leaf was critical to my journey.

From failing to pack lettuce correctly all the way to selling the business, sweating the small stuff helped me build the depth of skills I needed to run this business. And not to forget the emotional strength needed to be resilient when facing the inevitable ups and downs.

I hope you gained as much from reading this book as I did from writing it. It was a learning process to reflect and write about my experiences and highlight all the little things I did at the beginning that helped make the company a success as we expanded.

Through my time at Green Leaf, I transitioned from being an investor to becoming an entrepreneur, a manager, an operator, and even an amateur psychologist! It was the Plan, as I called it, but was not only a meaningful journey for my career but also for my life. Getting back to being an investor made me much more attuned to business challenges than I used to be.

Before, I would rely solely on quantitative information to make decisions. In a few short years, I gained a huge amount of business intuition and now, I can combine the hard data with a "gut-feel" for people and situations. This greatly improves outcomes.

That was all thanks to doing those small things in the early days of acquiring Green Leaf. It was not always easy or pleasant, but it accelerated my learning. More importantly, it renewed my appreciation for business and its force for good when channeled the right way. We employed over two hundred people in two countries. That's two hundred families who counted on Nijhad and I every day to make the right choice so the business would not only sustain them, but grow.

* * *

Today, I am back in the investing world with a focus on acquiring businesses in Sub-Saharan Africa, and I get to put the lessons I learned into practice every day. I can assess a business's capacity for change by talking to its middle management. A few minutes speaking to key heads of departments gives me a glimpse of the challenges and opportunities that business is facing. By asking the floor staff whether they know the company's vision or mission statement, I can understand if the entire firm is aligned with a dedicated strategy.

Finding a business with low resiliency or capacity to change is not inherently good or bad, but as an active investor looking to grow a business, your ability to gauge the difficulty surrounding, and receptiveness to, change will make all the difference.

The world around us is moving ever faster, so the company you lead needs to be able to adapt almost as fast, but therein lies the contradiction. Before you can become a great investor and effect rapid change, you have to first slow down and take the time to build your intuition. Do the small, everyday things that teach you how the business works.

Whatever job you have today or company you work for, try your hand at being a cashier, a baker, a janitor, a truck driver, a salesperson—whatever position in the firm gives you the most exposure to customers and staff. In those trenches, you'll learn the most. By doing those small, sometimes inane, things repeatedly, you will learn to quickly identify the patterns and strengths that make the business tick.

Don't underestimate the tangible and intangible value of those small things either. Whether you are a seasoned entrepreneur, a founder of a new start-up, or a career company-person, figure out what really drives your business and the people behind it. It is time well spent.

I am grateful to have sat next to Professor Segel that night, listening to his stories about how his hard, on-the-ground work, paid off.

Before running Green Leaf, I was overly focused on the analytical side of business, relying on facts, figures, and data to tell me what I needed to know. Now I understand there is something even more powerful: leadership. If you can speak honestly, share your vision for the future with your team, and let them take the lead, you will achieve your mission faster and better than you could ever imagine.

The catch is they need to believe you. They need to know you understand their difficulties and obstacles. You can inspire confidence if you've done those things yourself and sweated the same way they do in their everyday roles. And once they do, watch how your business expands and things that felt hard and disheartening become easy and satisfying.

During my last semester at Harvard, I learned from Professor Christensen that doing the hard things, those that make you think and sweat, is not the easiest. He gave us hard case studies not to disenchant us but because he knew the importance of struggling with the work. The harder the obstacle, the more satisfied you feel overcoming it.

Not all my Green Leaf stories made it (we had opened a store in Arusha!), and not everyone I interacted with is described here (you are still an important part of my journey!), but that does not mean they were not memorable. It only means I hit my editor's word limit!

My time at Green Leaf was incredibly inspiring and humbling. It changed me in so many ways, both as a professional and personally. I will be forever thankful to Nijhad for buying me coffee that fall day in New York, and to everyone in Tanzania and Kenya who looked out for Neha and me in this journey and helped make Dar our home for four years.

The people made it all worth it.

ALL OF RAM'S TIPS

CHAPTER 1

- Be clear about your investment criteria. Take your time to do the research and figure out your competitive advantage.

- Don't let your emotions dictate the price.

- Always raise more money than you think you need. And whatever you do, don't raise less.

- Don't underestimate the importance of building relationships when starting a new business. Even a random connection can help, but it's nothing if you don't put in the hard work and effort.

- People judge a book by more than its cover. Talk not only about your plan but also about yourself, what moves you, and why you are doing what you are doing.

- If you want something done and it's critical to your business, don't outsource it. Do it yourself.

- Treat all your stakeholders with respect and they will take care of you.

- Make sure to write down all the mistakes you made along the way. That way you can avoid repeating them later!

CHAPTER 2

- Sharing your goals can be daunting, but it doesn't have to be. Rehearse them, poke holes, share with a close group of family and friends first to test it out before broadcasting it to a larger audience. In the end, you will have to trust that it is the right thing for you.

- Being nervous is good because it can help you crystallize your thought process.

CHAPTER 3

How do you know you're making a good investment?
- It has to get you excited.

- It should match your personal and professional goals.

- You have to have a positive gut feel about it.

- It has to make money!

- Diligence it thoroughly. It is especially reassuring when your customers (no matter how few they are today) love the product. This will form the backbone of your vision for the business.

- Make sure to buy it at a reasonable price, without getting carried away by your emotions.

CHAPTER 4

- Five steps to set up an effective partnership:

    - Communicate at all times

    - Establish clear roles and responsibilities

    - Write out your goals and align your vision

    - Be open with each other

    - Make time to be friends

CHAPTER 5

- In the beginning, just ask, watch, and learn. If people want your opinion or a decision from you, resist the urge.

- When identifying problems, think about the root cause.

- When identifying solutions, consider whether that fix is scalable.

CHAPTER 6

- To figure out what the company is about, start with where it came from. By understanding its history, you can better chart its future.

- Make sure to understand how others perceive your company. Speak to your staff, customers, suppliers, and the surrounding community. They will give you different perspectives of the value you bring them.

- Don't underestimate the power of a mission statement and a vision. The larger the company, the more important it is to spread your culture.

- Being management does not make you superior. Make sure your line staff knows that. By avoiding this perception, it will motivate everyone to focus on the main task at hand: getting more sales!

CHAPTER 7
- Sweat the small stuff! Go all in to really understand how operations work at all levels of the company.

- Don't make assumptions upfront about what you think works or doesn't, what you can or should improve. Let yourself be guided by the work and the process. After all, if things are done a certain way, there must be a reason. Figure out the reason and then decide what to do.

- Earning trust is not easy, but it's the key to being a successful leader.

CHAPTER 8

- Don't forget about work-life balance, ideally before burn-out sets in! It's important to take time away from the business; incidentally, it will also provide perspective on what really matters (business-wise and personally).

CHAPTER 9

- Finding ways to accelerate communication will encourage the spread of best practices across the company.

- A manager can exhibit five types of power: positional, coercive, reward, expert, and referent. Figure out which ones you have and which you need to work on.

- To gain influence as a leader, build trusting relationships within the company, be the change you want to implement, be a lovable star, and project warmth and competence.

- Don't play the blame game. Use the concept of advocacy and inquiry, and the Ladder of Inference, to find ways to move forward.

- Use all of the above in your leadership meetings to pursue your goals!

CHAPTER 10

- Don't be afraid of failing, and don't be afraid of giving it your all. We all get challenged beyond our capabilities, but those moments push us to become better than we thought possible.

  – Fear of failure should never dictate your decisions.

- When you hear of inappropriate behavior in your company, trust, but verify.

- Difficult conversations are, by nature, difficult. Find ways to make them easier by choosing a neutral location, for example.

- Being a leader means making some tough decisions. Once a decision is made, don't second-guess, but be sure to have a clear rationale that underpins it and explain that to the rest of your team.

- Entrepreneurs, by nature, like to control and are reluctant to trust. Learn to let go of those instincts and trust those around you.

- Stay true to your values. In the long run, they matter more than your profits.

CHAPTER 11
- When looking to make changes, prioritize your improvements. Where will you get the biggest bang for your buck?

  - Focus on working with your current partners. After all, they have the most to lose if you move your business elsewhere. They can even be a good source of ideas for you!

- Don't be afraid to ask. In negotiations, you don't get what you don't ask for.

- If your first idea fails, try again. Try until you find the idea that sticks.

CHAPTER 12

- If you're setting up a new department or division, learn from others who have already gone through the process. If necessary, hire consultants or advisors. This will greatly accelerate your learning and prevent you from making easily avoidable mistakes.

  - External advisors can also help improve an existing department and bring you best practices or innovative problem-solving techniques.

  - Make sure those advisors understand your business model and can work within your constraints. Interview them like you were going to hire them!

- If someone says it can't be done, understand why first and see if you can challenge those assumptions. Sometimes it requires creative problem-solving.

- If you're starting something new that you're unsure about, think about starting small to minimize the money spent and effort expended.

- When interviewing, see if you can test the candidate live for their job skills.

CHAPTER 13

- Learn what the three financial statements (income statement, balance sheet, cash flow statement) can tell you about your business.

- Remember the importance of working capital. There's a difference between being profitable (making money on paper) and being solvent (having the cash to pay your staff and suppliers).

- If you're changing a system, process, or software, test it first on a small scale before implementing it.

- For a change process to be effective, follow these eight steps:

  - Establish a sense of urgency

  - Form a powerful guiding coalition

  - Create a vision

  - Communicate the vision

  - Empower others to act on the vision

  - Plan for and create short-term wins

  - Consolidate improvements and produce still more change

  - Institutionalize new approaches

- Connect the dots: inventory checks led to performance management roll-out!

- Trust bridges the gap between being an effective manager and becoming a successful leader.

CHAPTER 14

- Be available for your staff. Keeping an open-door policy helps you get information faster about what is going in the business.

- You can't control what the government or external stakeholders will do next, but you can prepare yourself.

CHAPTER 15

- Market research:

  - Read any public information you can find.

  - Subscribe to online local newspapers of the city in question.

  - Meet as many people as you can and let them talk.

  - Firsthand observation is key.

- Negotiations:

  - Be objective about pros and cons.

- Be transparent about what you can and cannot do.

- Be creative. Understand what the other side wants and see if you can reconcile with what you need.

- Don't let emotions dictate the price.

• Getting a loan:

- Let your passion and emotion show.

- Numbers need to be explained with a story.

- Show the work you've done to get there.

CHAPTER 16

• When expanding your business:

- Don't be afraid to rethink certain aspects (like the design or layout). If you can improve on the status quo, do it.

- Stick with your vision and mission statement. Let them guide what you change and what you keep.

- Test and retest to make sure you're ready before the big day.

- Don't rush unless you're ready, and don't let feelings of hubris or complacency make you skip critical steps in the process.

- Building a new team:

  - Find a culture carrier who can be a bridge between the old and the new.

  - The first employees are critical. No matter the level, be involved in the interview process. This will set the right tone and help emphasize your culture.

  - When hiring, focus on attitude more than on experience. It's easier to train people in the way you want things done than to change someone's mindset into a hard worker.

  - In the same vein as interviewing, make sure you're part of the training.

- Building partnerships:

  - Understand your partner(s) experiences and motivation. Make sure they are aligned with yours.

CHAPTER 17

- Combat loneliness in your work. You can't single-handedly change your company, grow it, and lead a team effectively.

- Beware the financial and health stress of managing and growing a business. There is a personal cost in achieving success.

- Lifestyle Business vs. Building an Empire. You can choose to run a business as is without taking outside investment or reinvesting. If you want to build a larger company, you will need to constantly reinvest or even raise outside capital to grow locations and stores.

- Financial investors can turbocharge your growth, but they are short term by nature. Keep in mind their investment horizon when looking to raise funds from them, and make sure it is appropriate for your business and vision.

CHAPTER 18

- Raising money from family and friends is tedious and emotionally challenging. You can do it in the early stages, but when you need to grow fast, this is not the best avenue.

- Financial investors can provide you a large amount of capital to grow quickly and hire more people. However, they are often constrained by short-term horizons. In many regions and sectors, this model has proven inappropriate.

- Family investors or corporations, on the other hand, can take a longer-term view or generational approach. They are willing to invest when conditions are difficult and wait for things to improve to reap the rewards.

- Finding an investor is like finding the right partner: understand if there is a fit with your business and culture.

CHAPTER 19

- Always plan more time than you think is needed for a transition.

  – Be honest and transparent to your staff about why you're leaving.

  – Keep a positive tone. The best sign of your positive contribution is that the company continues to thrive after you're gone.

  – Strive to leave things better than when you found them.

- It's ok to be emotional in business. If you need to second-guess your decision, do it and make sure it "feels right." This is a critical part of building your intuition!

- If your original plan doesn't work, it's ok! Find an alternative and make the best of it.

ACKNOWLEDGMENTS

—

This book would not have been possible without the support and love of so many people.

First to those who believed in my book even before I had finished the first draft. I am sincerely grateful for your support, pre-orders, and help in spreading the word.

Sarah Allibhoy

Pierre Anglès d'Auriac

Vikram Arora

Simran Bindra

Clayton Bohle

Rebecca Burton

Sekou Calliste

Joyce Chan

Clive Chang

Aalia Chatur

Alberto Chocron

Morris Chynoweth

David Damiba

Adam Davies

Vanessa De Carvalho

Margarita de la Piedra

Ola El-Shawarby

Álvaro Febrel

James Flanagan

Julien Garcier

Saket Gautam

Frédéric Genta

Olivier Granet

Sarah Grant

Daniel Gwak

Andrea Hestvik

Philip Hestvik

Bonga Hlongwane

Caroline Hofmann

Kevin Hong

Scott Hughes

Phoebe Hung

Rabia Ibtasar

Matt Isenhower

Sola Jagun

Nijhad Jamal

Jamila Jamani

Clementine James

Akshay Javeri

Niraj Javeri

Shabrina Jiva

Austin Johnsen

Claude Kamga

Omar Khan

Eu Wen Khoo

Maheen Saleem Khosa

Caroline Kim

Dan Klinck

Eric Koester

Jennifer Krusius

Alok Kumar

Ankit Kumar

Rashmi Kumar

Daniel Lambert

Rangassamy Lokan

Kyle Lui

Richard Lund

Barbara Magid

Puneet Mahajan

Jessica Mahoney

Cristin Marona

Jerome Masson-Roy

Becky May

Catherine McRoy-Mendell

Matthew Mendell

Anu Menon

Isaac Middelmann

Carlos Roberto Montesinos

Pierre-Etienne de Montgrand	Nupur Sadiwala
Serge Mouracade	Miguel Sanchez
Karina Nagin	Ajay Shah
Nandini Nayar	Radha Shah
Nobuhle Ndlovu	Ramya Shah
Brendan Negroni	Ravi Shah
Catalin Obogeanu	Aparna Shewakramani
Brendan O'Grady	Suyin Soon
Nicolas Opie	Claire Steiner
Nupur Parikh	Daniel Tai
Shamik Patel	Rob Teahen
Hayk Piloyan	Helina Teklehaimanot
Brian Polsinello	Vimal Vaghmaria
Natasha Prasad	Anne Vigier
Tim de Raedt	N. Vijayakumar
Nicholas Renart	Justin Walsh
Lasse Ristolainen	Delon White
Dimiti Rouil	Irene Yu
Matthew Ruban	Yan Zhao

Thank you, Marie, for sharing the joys and pains of the writing process. And thank you to Professor Eric Koester and the entire team at New Degree Press for making sure I included enough emotional depth, dialogues, and descriptions!

A big thank you to my earliest readers—Ankit, Jessica, Matt, Catherine, and Robert—for reading the entire manuscript and for the kind words and honest feedback. A sincere thank you to everyone in Dar and Nairobi who helped Neha and I feel at home in East Africa. And to the Green Leaf team, you will always be like a second family to us. A wholehearted thank you to my family for their constant words of support, unconditional love, and for believing in me throughout this process. Thank you, Nijhad, for convincing me to embark on this amazing adventure. And thank you for reliving it all by reading the book multiple times and reminding me of what a great journey we shared!

Running a business was harder than I could have ever imagined, only slightly harder than writing a book. None of this would have been possible without my wife and best friend, Neha. Thank you for your invaluable support, constant counsel, incredible heart, continuous listening, and unbounded love. I wrote this book in the first person, but none of this journey would have been possible without you. I love you, always.

BIBLIOGRAPHY

INTRODUCTION

Christensen, Clayton M. *The Innovator's Dilemma: When New Technologies Cause Great Firms to Fail.* Boston: Harvard Business Publishing, 1997.

CHAPTER 1

Nobel, Carmen. "Why Companies Fail—and How Their Founders Can Bounce Back." *Harvard Business School Working Knowledge,* March 7, 2011. https://hbswk.hbs.edu/item/why-companies-failand-how-their-founders-can-bounce-back.

CHAPTER 7

Khan, Mozaffar and George Serafeim. "Accor: Designing an Asset-Right Business and Disclosure Strategy." *HBS Case Study* no. 9-115-036. Boston: Harvard Business School Publishing, 2015.

CHAPTER 8

International Monetary Fund. "World Economic Outlook Database, October 2019." Accessed September 19, 2020. https://www.imf.org/external/pubs/ft/weo/2019/02/weo-data/index.aspx.

CHAPTER 9

Baer, Drake. "How Changing One Habit Helped Quintuple Alcoa's Income." Business Insider, April 9, 2014. https://www.businessinsider.com/how-changing-one-habit-quintupled-alcoas-income-2014-4.

Cuddy, Amy. "Power and Influence." Lecture Presented at Harvard Business School, Boston, MA, Fall 2010.

Gardner, Heidi K. "Leadership and Organizational Behavior." Lecture Presented at Harvard Business School, Boston, MA, Fall 2009.

CHAPTER 11

Malet, Jean-Baptiste. *L'Empire de l'Or Rouge: Enquête Mondiale sur la Tomate d'Industrie.* Paris: Fayard, 2017.

CHAPTER 13

Kotter, John P. "Leading Change: Why Transformation Efforts Fail." *Harvard Business Review,* May-June 1995. https://hbr.org/1995/05/leading-change-why-transformation-efforts-fail-2.

Narayanan, V.G. "Financial Reporting and Control." Lecture Presented at Harvard Business School, Boston, MA, Fall 2009.

CHAPTER 17
Schwarzman, Stephen A. *What It Takes: Lessons in the Pursuit of Excellence.* New York: Simon & Schuster, 2019.